Designed for Humans

Rethinking work in the age of AI

Theo Smith

First published in 2026.

ISBN: 978-1-0369-5485-7

Designed for Humans: Rethinking Work in the Age of AI

To all those creative thoughts, ideas and dreams that never happen. They get lost in the river, taken away to the sea.

This is one idea that didn't get away, captured, written down and presented for you to see.

Never let other people wash away your dreams, set them free on to the page or into the sea, but never let others decide which it should be!

One day we too will wash to the sea, and there finally our dreams will be set free.

Contents

About the Author

I didn't arrive at this work through a neat academic pathway. I came to it through experience, and that experience wasn't always kind.

For much of my early work life, I looked like I was doing fine. In my first proper career choice after my stint as a professional Actor, I would deliver results, build systems, and found my own way to make things work.

What people couldn't see was the effort it took to survive systems that weren't designed for how I process information. I learned differently, often needing more time at the start, more explanation, more space to join the dots. Rather than ask for that, I created workarounds. It kept me afloat, but it cost me confidence, energy, and at times, my sense of belonging.

Those patterns weren't new. They echoed my experiences in education, being capable, but out of sync with the way things were taught or assessed. Now, I look back, on reflection, I realise the problem wasn't a lack of ability. It was that the systems around me were too narrow, too rigid, and too quick to confuse difference with deficit.

Today, I work with organisations, universities and governments around the world to help change that. I'm an award-winning author, international speaker, and consultant with over 15 years' experience across recruitment, talent, and leadership.

I've partnered with employers in the private, public, and academic sectors to redesign hiring, onboarding, and the development of systems and processes so people don't have to mask, overcompensate, or burn out just to succeed.

I host the podcast *Neurodiversity with Theo Smith*. Write and speak regularly on the future of work. I also spend much of my time in rooms with leaders who want to do better but aren't always sure where to start.

This book exists for them, and for anyone who has ever felt capable yet quietly overwhelmed by systems that didn't quite fit.

linkedin.com/in/theosmithuk

youtube.com/@NeurodiversityWithTheoSmith

How to Use This Book

This book isn't here to tell you how to be better at work.

It's here to help you see work more clearly.

Much of what we struggle with at work doesn't show up as a problem straight away. It shows up as effort, as coping; as people adapting quietly to systems that weren't designed with them in mind. Often, by the time something looks "wrong", the cost has already been paid by someone.

The chapters that follow are invitations to look underneath those patterns. To question what's been normalised. To notice where work asks people to bend, stretch, mask, or compensate; and where we've learned to treat that as just part of the job.

To help you pause, reflect, and notice what might otherwise stay invisible, you'll find a few recurring sections throughout the book.

Designed for Human Action

At the end of each chapter, you'll find a section called **Designed for Human Action**.

These aren't action plans. They're not instructions.

They're moments to slow down and notice.

Each one draws attention to the quieter consequences of how work is designed, the effort that goes unseen, the assumptions that go unchallenged, the behaviours that get labelled rather than understood. You don't need to change anything immediately.

Often, seeing the system more clearly is the work.

Conversation Starters

Each chapter also ends with a single **Conversation Starter**.

This is one question you can take into a team meeting, a one-to-one, a leadership discussion; or simply sit with yourself. They're designed to open up conversations that are usually avoided, rushed, or softened away.

Try to approach them with openness rather than defensiveness. They're not about blame. They're about understanding what the system is asking of people; and at what cost.

Signals to Notice & Other Reflection Prompts

In a few places, you'll also find simple reflection prompts, titled **One Small Experiment**.

These aren't there to fix anything. They're there to help you spot patterns: early warning signs, hidden effort, or moments where the system is quietly doing more work than it needs to.

Use them if they're helpful. Leave them if they disrupt your reading flow.

If you're reading this as a leader, manager, or HR professional, you may start to see patterns you're responsible for shaping. If you're reading as someone who's felt capable but quietly overwhelmed by work, I hope you find language for experiences that are often dismissed or misunderstood.

Most of all, use this book as a lens, not a manual. Let it help you notice what's been normalised, and imagine what could be different.

Who This Book Is For (and Not For)

This book is an invitation to look at work differently.

Not to fix people. Not to optimise behaviour. But to notice what our systems are quietly asking of humans, and who is paying the cost.

It will be most useful if you're reading it with curiosity rather than certainty.

This book is for you if:

- You sense that many so-called "people problems" at work aren't random, but part of a pattern
- You've watched capable people struggle, stall, or burn out and felt uneasy with the explanations you were given

- You manage, hire, lead, design processes, or influence decisions; and suspect that good intentions haven't been enough
- You're willing to question systems that may have worked well for you personally
- You want language for experiences that are often dismissed, minimised, or individualised

You don't need to be an expert in leadership, inclusion, or AI to read this book. You don't need to agree with everything in it either. What matters more is a willingness to notice patterns and sit with what they reveal.

This book is not for you if:

- You're looking for quick fixes, checklists, or a "top ten ways to be more inclusive" guide
- You want reassurance that performance problems are primarily about individual resilience, attitude, or effort
- You believe inclusion is about being nicer, softer, or lowering standards
- You're hoping AI will remove the need for human judgement, responsibility, or difficult conversations
- You want this book to confirm what you already believe, rather than challenge it

Those positions aren't malicious. They're common, often rewarded, and deeply normalised.

But they rest on assumptions this book is intentionally questioning.

Introduction

The world of work is buzzing with talk of artificial intelligence, automation, and the next big leap in productivity. Leaders are told that AI will transform everything, from how we hire to how we manage to how we measure success. But beneath the noise, a quieter, more urgent truth remains: we still haven't figured out the workplace for humans.

This book is for HR professionals, managers, and anyone curious about management through the lens of the employee experience. It's for leaders who want to do more than keep up with trends. They want to build organisations where people can truly thrive.

The reality is simple: humans work, humans think, humans buy, humans make, humans eat, humans breathe. Without the human context, we risk building a world of work that forgets its central figure, the human.

Technology can accelerate, optimise, and scale, but it cannot replace the need for workplaces designed with people in mind.

Too often, we treat people problems as individual failings, when in fact they are design problems. We inherit systems that reward sameness, demand endurance, and quietly exclude those who don't fit the mould. We chase efficiency, but rarely pause to ask: efficient for whom? At what cost?

As AI and automation reshape the landscape, the stakes are higher than ever. If we don't get the human element right, we risk scaling our failures instead of our successes. The future of work isn't just about smarter machines, it's about smarter, more humane systems.

This book invites you to rethink work from the ground up. It's not a manual or a manifesto. It's a lens, a way to see the familiar with fresh eyes, to question what we've normalised, and to make conscious choices about the kind of workplaces we want to build.

Because in the end, the most important innovation isn't artificial intelligence, it's remembering what makes work, and life, worthwhile: the human at the centre of it all.

Opening note

This book isn't about being nicer

Most workplaces don't set out to exclude people.

They set out to be efficient.

Predictable.

Consistent.

Over time, those priorities become systems. Systems that work well for some people, most of the time. And when they don't, the explanation is usually individualised.

"They're not quite a fit"

"They're struggling"

"They need to adapt"

Rarely do we pause to question the system itself.

This book exists because I've spent years watching that pattern play out quietly across organisations, sectors, and roles. In hiring. In onboarding. In management. In progression. In the way difference is tolerated right up until it becomes inconvenient.

People with squiggly careers, those without neat academic pathways, and those who were excluded early at school, in communities, or at work. They tend to feel the impact first. Not because they are more difficult, but because the margin for error is smaller. When work relies heavily on unspoken rules, social inference, and performance under pressure, the cracks don't take long to appear.

But those cracks don't only affect people on the edges.

They affect anyone who doesn't naturally mirror the system. Anyone who works differently. Anyone whose strengths don't present themselves in familiar ways.

This isn't a book about compliance.

It's not a manifesto.

And it's not an argument for lowering standards.

It's a book about how work has been shaped around assumptions that are rarely questioned. About how many of our so-called "people problems" are really design problems. And about what happens when we stop asking individuals to compensate for systems that were never built with them in mind.

And then there's the elephant in the room: AI.

We're on the brink of automating many of the very things we've been doing badly for over a hundred years. Decisions about hiring, performance, productivity, and potential, all of it, are increasingly being handed to systems built on the same old assumptions.

The uncomfortable truth is this: we haven't done a great job of getting the right people into the right roles, or supporting them once they're there. And now we're in danger of scaling those failures, quietly and efficiently, through automation.

You don't need to agree with everything in here.

You don't need to recognise yourself in every example.

And you don't need to fix everything at once.

You just need to decide where to start.

The chapters that follow can be read in order or dipped into individually. They're not instructions. They're lenses, ways of seeing familiar systems more clearly, so what happens next becomes a conscious choice rather than an inherited habit.

Once you start looking at work this way, it tends to change what you notice.

And from there, different choices become possible.

Before you begin: where responsibility sits

It's easy to read a book like this as observation.

To recognise patterns "out there".

To nod along, feel seen, and move on.

But workplaces don't design themselves.

They become what we repeat.

They set around what we tolerate.

They reward what we measure.

And they quietly teach people what it costs to belong.

If you manage people, hire them, promote them, set expectations, run meetings, shape workload, write policy, approve tools, or decide what "good" looks like; then you already have influence over the design.

This isn't about blame.

Most systems were inherited. Most choices once felt sensible.

But responsibility still lives with the people closest to the work; the people who can notice, revisit, and choose differently when the consequences become clear.

So here's the shift I'm inviting you to make as you read:

not "What's wrong with them?"

but "What is this system asking of people; and who is paying the cost?"

If you only take one thing from this book, let it be this:

when people struggle in predictable ways, it's rarely random.

It's feedback.

And feedback belongs to the design.

Chapter 1

When work only works for some

Most workplaces don't fail people with a bang.

It tends to happen quietly, and by then it's hard to trace back.

It happens through processes that feel vanilla, expectations that go unquestioned, and systems designed for efficiency long before they were designed for humans.

And when those systems don't work, we rarely question the design. We look at the individual instead.

Why can't they focus?

Why are they so sensitive?

Why do they struggle with deadlines, communication, meetings, confidence, or feedback?

We diagnose performance.

We rarely diagnose the system.

We live in a world of neurological diversity. Always have. Difference in how brains process information, manage energy, respond to stimuli, or make sense of complexity isn't new. It's how humans have adapted to different environments over time.

You can see this across nature. Take the Mexican tetra fish. When some populations moved into dark cave systems, sight stopped being useful. Over generations, those fish evolved without it. They lost their sight and eventually their eyes. What would look like a deficit in one environment became an adaptation in another.

The fish didn't fail. The context changed.

Human brains have evolved in much the same way. Different ways of noticing patterns, responding to noise, tolerating uncertainty, or conserving energy have always existed. The issue isn't difference. It's what happens when environments change faster than our assumptions about people.

The modern workplace is a strange setting for the human brain. Bright lights. Constant noise. Open offices. Endless digital communication. Speed rewarded over depth.

People packed into environments that demand sustained attention and rapid response, often without space to recover. It's no wonder some people struggle to fit into what is, in evolutionary terms, a very new and unnatural way of working.

Neurodiversity matters in this context because neurodivergence exposes this mismatch early. Not because anyone is "more difficult", but because some people have less margin to absorb unnecessary friction.

What others tolerate, compensate for, or quietly burn themselves out navigating, is often felt immediately. It isn't always named, shared, or even recognised as non-universal, but it's a signal that the system is asking too much of the person, not the other way around.

They don't break the system.

They reveal where it was already broken.

The pattern is rarely dramatic or sudden. Instead, it unfolds step by step, often invisibly, through the design of our systems.

The following steps illustrate how efficiency-driven workplaces can quietly lead to exclusion, burnout, and missed talent.

Systemic Exclusion Flowchart

- **Efficiency-driven priorities:** Speed, scale, defensibility become the primary goals.

- **Rigid systems and inherited assumptions:** Past decisions are treated as neutral truths rather than design choices.

- **One-size-fits-all processes:** Variation is removed in the name of consistency.

- **Hidden or unspoken rules emerge:** What really matters isn't written down, but people learn it quickly.

- **Cognitive and social friction increases:** More guessing, more self-monitoring, more invisible work.

- **Individuals adapt to survive the system:** Masking, over-compensating, performing confidence, staying silent.

- **Early signals are misread:** Anxiety becomes "lack of resilience". Withdrawal becomes "low engagement". Missed cues become "capability gaps".

- **Labels replace understanding:** "Not quite a fit". "Struggling". "Not ready yet".

- **Support arrives late or not at all**: Adjustments are reactive, gated, or framed as exceptions.

- **Burnout, attrition, and missed talent**: The system loses people it never truly saw.

When we see exclusion as a systemic outcome, not an individual failing, new possibilities for change emerge.

The myth of the "problem person"

Across my work in recruitment, talent, HR, and leadership, I've seen the same story play out in different organisations, sectors, and roles.

A capable person joins, with genuine intent and optimism on both sides.

Early signs appear. Misunderstandings. Exhaustion. Missed cues. Anxiety. Frustration.

And so, performance conversations begin.

Support is offered, often kindly, but vaguely. Over time, confidence erodes. The person either leaves, is managed out, or stays, shrinking themselves to survive.

When the story is told internally, it sounds reasonable:

"They weren't quite right for the role"

"They struggled with the pace"

"They needed a lot of support"

"They just didn't fit how we work"

But when you zoom out, the same outcomes repeat with different people. That's the clue.

If the issue were individual capability, it would be rare and unpredictable.

When it's systemic, it becomes a pattern, and often that pattern is ignored.

We like to think neurodivergence is a "special case".

But the truth is, a lot of people are quietly struggling, just trying to make the system work for them.

And the reason it feels so hard isn't because difference is uncommon.

It's because the system is built to reward the people who fit the mould.

We have normalised endurance and called it competence.

When good intentions aren't enough

The hardest thing about inclusion is that most people mean well and still, it doesn't work.

I work with leaders and HR teams who care. They spend time and money on it. They go to training. They write policies. They launch initiatives. They really try.

And yet, the outcomes don't change.

People still burn out.

Employees still stall or leave.

Adjustments still arrive late, if they arrive at all.

Managers still feel unsure, unsupported, and stuck.

This is where inclusion conversations often fall apart, because intent gets confused with impact.

When organisations assume that caring is the same as designing well, any challenge starts to feel like an accusation.

But this book isn't a call-out; it's a design conversation.

You can care deeply and still be relying on systems that quietly exclude.

You can have the best intentions in the world and still be asking people to adapt to environments that were never designed with them in mind.

That doesn't make you malicious.

It makes you human, working inside systems you inherited.

So the question isn't, *"Do we care?"*

It's *"What have we normalised without ever questioning it?"*

Neurodiversity didn't create these problems

Neurodiversity didn't invent burnout.

It didn't invent poor management.

It didn't invent unclear expectations, performative culture, or bad hiring decisions.

What it did was give us language for patterns that already existed.

Long before neurodiversity entered corporate vocabulary, organisations were losing capable people in predictable ways.

They hired for confidence and presence rather than skill.

They rewarded people who could tolerate ambiguity rather than those who could solve problems.

They designed roles around output without thinking about energy, cognition, or sustainability.

Neurodiversity simply made the cracks visible.

AI has accelerated the need for organisations to confront them.

When someone can't mask, compensate, or conform without cost, the system gets exposed faster. Meetings that rely on unspoken rules. Roles that demand constant context-switching without recovery. Performance measures that prioritise visibility over value.

The issue isn't that neurodivergence demands or needs "special treatment".

The issue is that we've built systems that assume one way of thinking, communicating, and coping.

And then we act surprised when people struggle.

The slow erosion of high performers

One of the most damaging myths in work is that high performers don't struggle.

In reality, many of the people who stay the longest in poorly designed systems are those who are quietly burning themselves out to keep up. They over-prepare. They work longer hours. They compensate in ways that aren't visible.

From the outside, they look fine.

From the inside, they are exhausted.

I've spoken to countless people who didn't realise how much energy work was costing them until something broke.

Health, confidence, and identity. They blamed themselves for not being resilient enough, not organised enough, not "professional" enough.

What they were actually responding to was constant cognitive friction.

When work demands sustained self-regulation, interpretation, masking, and recovery, performance becomes expensive. Some people can afford that cost for longer than others. That doesn't make them better. It makes the system more selective than it needs to be.

High performance achieved through constant self-sacrifice is not sustainable performance.

It's deferred failure. We see this in the performance of start-up and scale-up organisations, as much as we see it in employees. They hit a performance wall because of burnout.

This is why high performers are often the last to be protected. Their resilience is read as capacity, and their adaptability becomes permission for the system to ask for more.

Over time, coping is mistaken for sustainability, and erosion happens quietly. From the outside, everything looks fine, right up until it isn't. That's why "they seemed fine" is such a familiar post-exit story. The system did exactly what it was set up to do.

I've seen this from both sides. As a consultant, and earlier in my own career.

In my early recruitment roles, I looked like I was coping. I built parallel systems outside the company tools so the work still got done, but it meant extra effort, hidden strain, and problems that only showed up later.

The truth was, I learn systems differently: I might take longer at the start, but once I've got it, I see patterns and opportunities others miss.

I stopped asking for things to be explained again because it felt like being back at school; the naughty one who didn't get it straight away.

That silence cost me confidence, trust, and nearly my career, not because I lacked ability, but because the system never adapted.

How adjustments became a tick-box

Workplace adjustments were never meant to be exceptional.

They were meant to be ordinary, part of how work adapts to humans, not the other way around.

But that's not how they show up in practice.

I saw this clearly while auditing a health and social care organisation in the UK. At the time, they were dealing with a long list of challenges. Processes were creaking. People were stretched. Inclusion was something they cared about, but didn't yet know how to embed.

I spent months inside the organisation, reviewing systems, policies, and documentation. I interviewed staff. I ran surveys. I built the case for neuroinclusion and how it could be designed into the fabric of the organisation.

They later went on to be recognised as a European Top Employer.

But at the start, the picture was very different.

One finding stopped everyone in their tracks.

Around **30% of employees said they were facing neurological barriers to performing well in their role**. That's not a fringe issue. That's nearly a third of the workforce quietly struggling.

And yet, only **10% of employees had ever asked for a reasonable adjustment**.

Almost every single one of those requests was for flexible working hours.

Not one person had asked for support with processing information.

Not one had requested technology to assist with reading or writing.

Not one had asked for adaptations that could have reduced errors, prevented burnout, or made the role more sustainable over time.

This was a health and social care provider, responsible for caring for older adults. The idea that no one needed support with information processing, communication, or cognitive load simply didn't add up.

So the question wasn't, *"Do people need adjustments?"*

They clearly did.

The real question was: why didn't they feel able to ask?

This is where adjustments quietly become a tick-box.

In theory, support exists. In practice, it arrives late, framed as a favour, and wrapped in discomfort. People are asked to disclose, justify, and explain themselves before help appears.

Managers worry about fairness.

HR worries about precedent.

The individual worries about being seen as difficult, needy, or less capable.

By the time adjustments are discussed, trust has already been eroded.

That's not because anyone is acting in bad faith.

It's because inclusion has been bolted on, rather than designed in.

When systems assume one default way of working, anyone outside that default becomes an exception.

Exceptions create friction.

Friction creates reluctance.

Reluctance creates delay.

And delay creates harm.

But when flexibility is designed into systems from the start, adjustments stop feeling special. They stop being something you have to *ask* for. They become part of the infrastructure.

Clear expectations.

More than one way to communicate.

Predictable processes.

Choice, where possible.

These aren't "inclusive initiatives".

They're just good design principles.

And when they're in place, something important happens: people don't have to fight the system to do their best work.

This isn't about lowering standards

A concern I hear often, sometimes spoken and sometimes implied, is this:

"If we make changes, do we lower the bar?"

The answer is no.

But we do need to be honest about what the bar is actually measuring.

Many systems claim to assess ability while rewarding performance under very specific conditions. Fast thinkers, confident speakers, people comfortable with ambiguity, and people who can navigate unspoken expectations.

That isn't a neutral measure of capability. It's a measure of how well someone fits a particular environment.

Designing work for humans doesn't mean reducing expectations. It means aligning them with what actually matters in the role, rather than relying on shortcuts that are easier to observe than to justify.

When systems are designed with that clarity, something interesting happens. Performance improves without people being infantilised, singled out, or quietly excluded. The same changes that support disabled or neurodivergent people often make work easier for everyone else.

Not because standards were lowered.

But because friction was removed.

A different starting point

This book isn't asking you to become an expert in neurodiversity.

Or disability.

Or race.

Or gender.

Or any one facet of human variation.

It's asking something more practical than that.

It's asking you to become curious about the systems you rely on.

Where do people struggle most?

Where does effort consistently outweigh outcome?

Where do the same issues repeat, even as the individuals change?

Those are design questions, not performance ones.

Neurodiversity is one useful lens, but it isn't the only one. It helps us see where work demands a particular way of thinking, communicating, or coping, and quietly penalises those who don't match it. The same lens often reveals barriers that affect far more people than we initially expect.

If we start there, the conversation shifts.

From "What's wrong with them?"

to "What is this system asking of people?"

From blame to responsibility.

From compliance to intention.

Most workplaces don't need a radical overhaul.

They need more honest attention to how work actually operates.

That's where this book begins.

Designed for Human Action

(Where to notice before you redesign)

This chapter isn't asking you to change anything yet.

It's asking you to notice what you've learned to treat as normal.

Most exclusion doesn't start with policies.

It starts with assumptions that feel sensible because they're familiar.

Before you redesign anything, it's worth pausing here.

Notice what you've learned to explain away

Listen for the phrases that quietly close conversations.

"They're just not a good fit"

"They struggle with the pace"

"They're capable, but..."

On their own, these sound reasonable.

Over time, they become familiar.

When the same explanations appear across different people, teams, or roles, they stop being individual judgements.

They become patterns.

And patterns are rarely about people.

They're about systems doing what they were designed to do.

Notice what gets treated as "normal"

Without judgement, start paying attention to what success seems to require here.

Who finds it easiest to thrive?

What ways of thinking are rewarded without being named?

Which kinds of effort are expected, but never acknowledged?

Normal and *typical* aren't impartial. They exclude by design.

Shaped by the systems we inherit, reuse, and rarely question.

Once something is labelled "just how things work", it stops being examined, even when it quietly excludes people who don't fit the mould.

A thought to carry forward

If a workplace only works well for people who think, communicate, and cope in similar ways, that's not coincidence.

That's design.

And design can be changed, but only once we're willing to see it clearly.

That's what this book is really asking you to do.

· · ·

Conversation Starter

Each chapter, I'll offer you one question to take back to your next team meeting, catch-up, or simply to reflect on yourself.

Try to be as open, self-critical, and honest as you can. These questions are designed to quietly stretch the systems we've let design themselves without question for far too long.

If you want to spark a real conversation in your team, try this question:

> *"What's one part of our workplace that quietly asks people to adapt, rather than adapting to them?"*

Before you move on:

Here are some signals I've seen in organisations where design problems go unnoticed.

Use this checklist to reflect on your own workplace.

You don't need to fix anything yet, just notice what's present.

Signals to Notice (For Leaders)

- Fewer questions in meetings, or team members who stop challenging assumptions
- High performers who seem "fine" but later burn out or disengage
- "Unwritten rules" that only insiders seem to know
- Feedback that's met with silence, not discussion
- Support or adjustments that arrive only after a crisis, not before
- Repeated use of phrases like "not a good fit" or "struggling" in performance reviews
- Team energy spent on navigating process or politics, rather than on meaningful work

As a leader, which of these signals have you noticed in your team or organisation? What might they be telling you about the systems you're responsible for?

Chapter 2

When work doesn't fit: a human story

For a long time, nothing was obviously wrong.

That, in hindsight, was part of the problem. When nothing is visibly wrong, there's nothing to question. No trigger for support. No reason to slow down or look underneath the surface. Progress becomes proof that the system works, even when the person inside it is quietly paying a cost nobody else can see.

On paper, things were fine. Better than fine, in some cases. I was working, progressing, being trusted with responsibility. I wasn't failing, falling behind, or standing out in ways that triggered concern. If you had looked at my CV or performance reviews, you wouldn't have seen a problem.

And yet, work always seemed to cost me more than it should.

Not in ways that were easy to explain. Not in ways that showed up in output. But in energy, recovery time, and the constant effort of holding things together. I didn't struggle to do the work. I struggled with what the work demanded alongside it.

That distinction matters more than we usually admit.

The quiet cost of coping well

One of the most misleading ideas we have about work is that if someone is performing, they must be fine.

Performance, after all, is visible. It's measurable. It reassures organisations that things are working as intended. But performance tells us nothing about the cost at which it is achieved.

For me, work required a level of constant self-regulation that I assumed was normal.

Monitoring how I came across. Preparing more than others seemed to need to. Replaying conversations in my head long after they ended, and long into the night. Recovering from meetings in ways I didn't have language for at the time.

I didn't frame this as a problem; I framed it as professionalism.

If work felt draining, that was on me to manage. If I felt out of sync, that was something to work on. If certain environments exhausted me, the assumption was that I needed to toughen up, adapt better, or simply try harder.

I needed to get into work earlier, leave later, and just work harder!

So I did.

And because I could, the system never had to change.

From the outside, it looked like I was coping.

Inside, it cost me more than I realised at the time. Meetings left me exhausted in ways I couldn't explain. The effort was constant, even when nothing looked wrong from the outside. I struggled to manage my energy levels, and that meant, my battery was quickly depleted.

What made this harder was not knowing who, if anyone, it was safe to talk to about it.

Workplaces often say they take mental health seriously, but trust is built through people, not policies.

Without someone you recognise yourself in, someone you believe will understand rather than minimise, silence becomes the safest option.

The result isn't a lack of need; It's a lack of early

intervention. By the time support appears, the cost has already been absorbed.

It's taken me over 35 years to realise that my energy levels played such a significant role in my cognitive ability and that they were drained by what was happening around me and to me.

At some point, in my younger years at school and into the workplace, I had to make a choice. I stopped asking for things to be clarified. I adapted. I masked. I subconsciously told myself this was just what life and work required.

This is one of the most damaging dynamics in modern work: when people cope well enough to stay, their struggle becomes invisible.

The organisation sees output and assumes sustainability. The individual absorbs the cost and assumes it's personal.

Over time, that gap widens.

Learning the rules without being taught

Much of what made work difficult wasn't the tasks themselves; it was the invisible layer around them.

The unspoken expectations.

The tone you were meant to strike.

When it was acceptable to ask questions.

How confident was confident enough.

These weren't written anywhere; you were expected to pick them up through observation, inference, and trial and error.

I learned quickly that work wasn't just about doing your job; it was about performing work in the right way, saying the right things in the right order, with the right level of certainty.

Knowing when to speak and when to hold back. Knowing which parts of yourself were welcome, and which were best kept out of sight.

None of this was framed as masking at the time; it was framed as maturity.

And to be clear, this isn't unique to neurodivergent people; everyone learns some version of these rules. The difference is how much energy it takes to comply with them, and how forgiving the system is when you don't.

When you grasp these rules easily, they feel natural. When you don't, they feel like a test where the rules only become clear after you've already failed.

Success as a delaying factor

One of the reasons it took me so long to make sense of this is that I was succeeding.

That sounds counterintuitive, but it's a pattern I see repeatedly now. Success can delay the moment we stop and ask whether the system actually fits.

It gives us just enough external validation to ignore internal strain. It encourages us to attribute discomfort to ambition, pressure, or the normal demands of adult life.

If you're struggling and failing, people pay attention.

If you're struggling and succeeding, you're expected to carry on.

I didn't question whether the system fit me, because the system appeared to be rewarding me. Any sense of misalignment was reframed as something to manage privately.

That's why so many high performers don't recognise the cost they're paying until they can no longer pay it. Burnout doesn't arrive suddenly. It accumulates.

And when it does arrive, it often gets misdiagnosed as a resilience issue, a motivation problem, or a personal weakness. Rarely do we ask whether the system demanded something unnecessary in the first place.

Finding language later, not first

I didn't start this work because I was searching for an identity label; I started it because I kept seeing the same patterns.

I saw people who were clearly capable, intelligent, and committed, but who were exhausted by environments that others seemed to tolerate with ease.

Candidates who fell out of processes that claimed to be fair, and leaders who carried a disproportionate cognitive load without understanding why.

Neurodiversity gave language to things I was already observing. It didn't create the insight; it clarified it.

I've often been told I use the "wrong" language when talking about myself; that I identify incorrectly, that I should say I *have* something, rather than *am* something. What's always struck me is how confidently people I've never met feel able to correct my own experience.

That dynamic mirrors work more closely than we like to admit.

The rules, the labels, the "right" way to describe things are usually set by those who don't carry the cost of getting them wrong.

For me, language was never about grammar or

correctness; it was about finding words that felt true enough to stop pretending everything was fine.

That distinction matters because it keeps the conversation grounded in work design rather than diagnosis.

This isn't about categorising people. It's about understanding how different brains interact with the same systems, and why those systems privilege some styles of thinking over others.

Once you see that, you can start to take positive and meaningful action to improve those systems.

Masking as adaptation, not deception

One of the most misunderstood aspects of human experience is masking.

It can be perceived as hiding, pretending, or even deceiving.

In reality, it's usually adaptive; a way of getting through environments that weren't built with you in mind.

For me, masking wasn't a conscious strategy. It didn't start with a decision.

It happened gradually.

You notice what gets rewarded and what doesn't:

Who gets praised for speaking up.

Who gets labelled *"difficult"* for asking questions.

Which parts of you land well, and which ones quietly create friction.

So you adjust.

You soften your language.

You rehearse responses before meetings.

You force eye contact, suppress fidgeting, and hold back questions that might slow things down.

Over time, you become fluent in what work expects from you, even when it doesn't come naturally.

The problem isn't that people mask; the problem is when systems rely on masking to function.

Masking takes effort. Real effort.

It draws on energy reserves that don't show up in performance reviews or productivity metrics. You don't see it in output, only in exhaustion.

Over time, masking shapes who gets to stay, who progresses, and who is seen as "easy to manage". Not because they're better at the job, but because they're better at blending in.

Workplaces rarely intend to create this pressure, but they often normalise one way of being, without noticing who is doing the adapting.

Some people can.

Some people can't.

Some people can; until they break.

Seeing the same story everywhere

What finally shifted this from a personal experience to a professional responsibility was repetition.

Not just in meetings or reports, but out in the world.

If you've ever stood at a bus stop, waited in a school playground, or queued for a coffee, you'll know what I mean. You don't have to try very hard to overhear people talking about work.

A manager who doesn't get it.

Hours that don't fit around childcare.

Feeling constantly behind, even though they're doing their best.

The quiet anxiety of trying to hold everything together.

These conversations are private, but they happen in

public. And whether you want to or not, you hear them. There's a volume to them; not loud, just constant.

Once I started paying attention, I realised how familiar these conversations were. I heard the same frustrations again and again; not just about work, but about life more broadly.

Parents talking about children struggling in school systems that weren't designed for them; about labels, meetings, exhaustion, and the feeling of always being on the back foot.

And then, almost without pause, I'd hear adults describing the *same kinds of barriers* in their workplaces.

Different settings, same dynamics.

What struck me wasn't how unusual these stories were; it was how normal they were, how often they came up outside of work, and how rarely they were spoken about inside it.

Because these are not conversations people feel able to have at work.

Somewhere between the bus stop and the office door, the story disappears. The struggles get edited out, the tone changes and people adjust how they speak, what they share, and what they admit to needing.

That's when it clicked.

I started seeing the same patterns everywhere, in candidates, colleagues, clients, and leaders. Different industries, different roles, same underlying dynamics. People blaming themselves for struggles that were entirely predictable once you understood the system they were operating in.

This wasn't about resilience or attitude; it was about design.

Workplaces had been built around assumptions that were rarely questioned; assumptions about communication, time, attention, confidence, and energy. Assumptions that suited some people perfectly and left others quietly adapting in the background.

And when those assumptions weren't met, we went looking for explanations that located the problem in the person, not the structure.

That gap, between what people say out in the world and what they feel able to say at work is not accidental; it's a signal.

And it's one we've been ignoring for far too long.

Reframing the experience

Looking back, the most important shift wasn't discovering a label; it was reframing the experience.

From "Why is this harder for me?"

to "What is this system asking of people?"

That shift removes shame without removing responsibility; it allows us to design better without lowering standards. It invites curiosity instead of blame.

This chapter isn't here to ask for sympathy; it's here to establish something more useful: perspective.

When work doesn't fit, the answer isn't always to push harder; sometimes it's to redesign the environment so effort aligns with outcome.

That's not a personal failing; it's a design challenge.

And once you start looking at work through that lens, everything else in this book starts to make sense.

Designed for Human Action

(If I hide behind this mask, maybe they'll leave me alone)

This chapter isn't about empathy;

it's about what happens when coping is mistaken for sustainability.

The work here isn't to fix people;

it's to notice what your systems are rewarding, and what they're quietly consuming.

Stop equating output with wellbeing

Performance and wellbeing are not the same thing;

they just happen to coexist for a while.

Someone can deliver and still be depleting themselves.

Someone can meet expectations while spending disproportionate energy just to stay level.

When systems only react once output drops, they are responding at the point of failure, not at the point of strain.

By then, the cost has already been paid; just not by the organisation.

Get curious about the cost, not just the result

Most workplaces ask some version of:

"How are they performing?"

A more revealing question sits underneath it:

"What does it cost this person to perform like this, here?"

You don't need to ask that out loud yet, but thinking it changes how you interpret behaviour.

Sudden withdrawal.

Over-preparation.

Reluctance to take on more, even when capability is obvious.

These aren't motivation problems;

they're signs of how much energy something is taking.

A question worth considering

If someone left tomorrow, would you say:

"We didn't see that coming"

Or would you recognise that the signs were always there;

they just looked like competence.

Because when we treat performance as "proof it's fine",

the pressure stays hidden until someone drops out of the system.

And by then, the system has already taught them the lesson it didn't mean to.

. . .

Conversation Starter:

"Can you recall a time when someone was labelled 'difficult'; and what might have been happening in the system around them?"

Chapter 3

What Well-Designed Work Actually Feels Like

There's a risk in writing a book about what's broken.

You can end up accidentally teaching the reader that dysfunction is normal.

So before we go any further, I want to name the alternative.

Not the utopian version.

Not the "we've got a wellbeing strategy" version.

The real one.

Because well-designed work doesn't feel like a perk; it feels like the absence of something you didn't realise you'd been carrying.

A lot of people only notice that weight when they leave a role and their body stops bracing for Monday.

We saw this clearly during the return to work after Covid.

People realised how much energy public transport had been taking from them before they even arrived.

How much effort it took to sit all day in a noisy, open-plan office, with no control over temperature, light, or space.

Some noticed they had fewer migraines once they weren't sitting under harsh light.

Others realised they weren't ending the day completely depleted just from getting home.

Not because the work had changed, but because the conditions around it had.

This chapter is a marker in the ground.

So when you read the next chapters and find yourself thinking, *"That's just how work is"*,

you've got something else to measure it against.

Clarity without the constant guesswork

Well-designed work feels clear in a way that's often underestimated.

Not rigid.

Not over-engineered.

Just clear enough that people aren't doing a second job alongside their actual one.

That second job is familiar to many people, even if they've never named it.

Working out what "urgent" really means this time.

Decoding messages that could be read three different ways.

Guessing what's being judged, because no one has said it out loud.

Trying to look confident while quietly unsure, because uncertainty is treated like a risk.

In poorly designed systems, this hidden work becomes normal. People learn to absorb it without complaint. Over time, the effort disappears from view, but the cost doesn't.

In well-designed environments, that guesswork shrinks.

Not because people are more capable, but because the system stops asking them to infer so much.

I've seen this play out most clearly outside traditional HR conversations, in the design of physical space.

During the development of the BBC's Cardiff broadcast centre, the team deliberately explored how the building would be experienced by people who process sensory information differently. Using virtual reality, designers and decision-makers were shown what a typical office could feel like for someone who is neurodivergent.

Flickering lights that felt unbearable.

Visual clutter that made it hard to find your bearings.

Patterns that appeared to move.

Signage that blurred rather than guided.

It wasn't subtle. A few minutes was enough to understand how disorientating supposedly "normal" environments can be.

What followed wasn't a set of special features or bolt-on adjustments; it was a series of simple, intentional design choices.

Each floor was colour-coded, not just on signs, but through furnishings and finishes. When you step out of the lift, you know you're on the right floor without checking, remembering, or asking.

Open spaces exist, but with curtains and adaptable boundaries, so they can change depending on what people need in that moment. Lighting levels were reduced below standard office norms to avoid constant visual strain. Quiet spaces are distributed throughout the building rather than hidden away or treated as exceptional.

Most people walking into the building don't notice any of this.

And that's the point.

The building still feels energetic, professional, and collaborative.

The standards didn't drop.

The design didn't become clinical or restrictive.

What changed was how much effort people had to expend just to manoeuvre around the building.

The space stopped demanding constant interpretation.

People could focus on their work instead of managing the environment around it.

This is what an inclusive work environment looks like when it's designed rather than explained.

Not more instructions.

Not more resilience.

Just fewer moments where people are left guessing what the system expects of them.

And when that guessing disappears, something important happens.

Energy returns.

Confidence stabilises.

People stop over-preparing to protect themselves from misunderstanding.

Being clear doesn't mean there's less to do; it means you can actually do it without wearing yourself down.

Trust that doesn't require proof of suffering

In poorly designed workplaces, trust is often conditional.

You're trusted once you've shown you can cope.

You're trusted once you've made it obvious you're committed.

You're trusted once you've proved you'll bend yourself around the system without making a fuss.

That's not trust. That's compliance.

In well-designed work, trust is visible in the small choices people are allowed to make without negotiation.

How they plan their day.

How they approach a task.

How they communicate when something is unclear.

How they manage their energy without needing to justify it like a medical claim.

It's not that standards are lower, but the organisation stops confusing effort with value.

When trust is real, people stop spending so much time trying to look like the right kind of employee, and start putting that energy into the work.

That's what a lot of organisations miss.

They think trust is a cultural value.

It's a design outcome.

Safety to contribute, not just to comply

Some workplaces are polite.

That's not the same as safe.

Safety is when you can say:

- "I'm not sure"
- "I need that explained again"
- "That meeting format doesn't work for me"
- "I think we're missing something"

...without feeling like you've just put your reputation at risk.

In well-designed work, the system doesn't only reward the loudest people, the fastest people, or the most socially fluent people.

It makes room for different cognitive styles to show up as contribution, not as inconvenience.

That might look like:

Decisions written down, not just spoken.

Agendas that aren't a surprise.

A culture where follow-up in writing is normal, not a sign someone "can't keep up".

Space for thinking that isn't instantly turned into a live debate.

This isn't about making everyone comfortable all the time.

It's about removing unnecessary social penalties.

Because when the penalty is high, people stop speaking.

And when people stop speaking, the organisation gets quieter, narrower, and less intelligent over time.

Sustainable pace, not constant recovery

Some organisations talk about burnout like it's weather.

"It's been a busy quarter"

"It's just one of those periods"

"It's the nature of the work"

But if the work constantly requires recovery, it's not a tough culture; it's a leaky system.

Well-designed work still has pressure, but pressure shouldn't become business as usual.

You can work intensely, as long as there's space to recover. Having clearer direction means less rework, and meetings don't have to be the time suck that leaves you catching up for the rest of the day.

The easiest way to spot this is simple:

In well-designed work, people don't spend their evenings recovering from the *process* of work.

They're tired because they worked, not because they survived.

High standards, lower friction

This is the point where people start to worry.

"If we make things easier, do we lower the bar?"

No.

What we do is stop pretending the bar is fair for everyone.

A lot of workplaces end up measuring the wrong things because they're easy to see.

Confidence gets mistaken for skill.

Speed gets mistaken for intellect.

Being visible gets mistaken for impact.

Endurance gets mistaken for commitment.

Good systems are honest instead.

They make expectations clear.

They focus on what actually matters.

They stop rewarding people for simply surviving chaos as if that were talent.

And here's the part leaders often miss:

When you remove unnecessary friction, you don't get less out of people; you get more.

Because they're not spending half their energy protecting themselves just to survive the system.

A quiet recalibration

If this chapter makes you think, "That sounds nice, but unrealistic", I'd challenge that gently.

It's not unrealistic.

It's just uncommon.

And it's uncommon because most systems weren't deliberately designed.

They were inherited, patched, scaled, and defended.

The rest of this book is about those systems.

Not to blame people, but to make it harder to keep calling design problems "people problems".

Once you've experienced well-designed work, it's obvious when the system is making people pick up the slack.

Designed for Human Action

(A quicker way to spot design issues)

Most workplaces can describe performance.

Far fewer can describe the **cost of performance**.

That's the lens to hold as you read the next chapters.

When someone is doing well, don't just ask, "Are they delivering?"

Ask, "What does it cost them to deliver like this, here?"

Because in poorly designed systems, the early warning signs often look like strengths:

- over-preparation that gets praised as diligence
- silence that gets read as professionalism

- long hours that get labelled commitment
- avoiding meetings that gets framed as independence

None of those are inherently bad.

But if the same coping behaviours keep showing up in the same parts of the organisation, that's not personality. That's a problem within the workplace.

Hold onto one simple contrast:

When work is designed well, effort turns into progress.

When work is designed badly, effort turns into **self-protection**.

You don't need to fix anything yet.

Just stop calling self-protection "normal".

Design Audit—Three Questions

Before you move on: If you're ready to look at your own organisation with fresh eyes, pause and consider these three questions. They're not a checklist or a prescription; just a prompt to notice what's often hidden in plain sight.

1. Where do people struggle most in our system? (*What patterns repeat, even as individuals change?*)

2. What effort is quietly absorbed, but rarely acknowledged? (*Who is compensating for friction, and how is it hidden?*)
3. What have we normalised without ever questioning it? (*What "just how things work" explanations close off deeper inquiry?*)

You don't need answers yet; just a willingness to notice.

Conversation Starter:

"When was the last time work felt easy, clear, or energising for you? What made that possible?"

One Small Experiment

Invisible Work Inventory

List three tasks or behaviours in your team that require extra effort but are rarely acknowledged.

- Who is doing this work?
- What patterns do you see?
- *How might your systems be quietly demanding more than you realise?*

Chapter 4

Hiring: how capable people are filtered out before interviews

Most organisations believe their hiring processes are fair.

They are structured.

They are documented.

They are consistent.

And yet, the same complaints surface again and again after people are hired.

"We can't find the right talent"

"They looked great in the interview"

"They're not quite what we expected"

"We've had to manage another one out"

If hiring were as objective as we like to think, the outcomes wouldn't be this familiar.

It doesn't fail at random; it fails in the same places, over and over again.

The uncomfortable truth is that many hiring systems are doing exactly what they were designed to do. They're just not designed to find the best people. They're designed to find the most familiar faces.

Hiring doesn't fail at the interview stage

When organisations talk about inclusive hiring, they often focus on interviews: panel composition, question structure, bias training.

Those things matter, but they come too late.

Most exclusion happens long before anyone sits in a room or logs onto a call.

It happens in job design.

In job adverts.

In screening criteria.

In assumptions about what "good" looks like.

By the time candidates reach interview, the system has already filtered heavily, and the people most likely to be filtered out are often those who would have performed well once hired.

Not because they lack skill, but because they don't navigate application processes in the expected way.

The system mistakes difference in approach for lack of capability, and never gets the chance to be proven wrong.

Job descriptions as exclusion tools

Job descriptions are rarely written to describe the work. They're written to protect organisations from risk, to satisfy internal stakeholders, or to describe an idealised person who has never existed.

I've lost count of how many job adverts I've read that include phrases like "excellent communication skills" or "must thrive in a fast-paced environment", without ever explaining what that actually looks like in practice.

These phrases are copied from role to role, organisation to organisation, treated as common sense rather than design choices.

Long lists of requirements.

Vague expectations.

Inherited language no one questions.

"Fast-paced"

"Resilient"

"Excellent communicator"

"Must be able to juggle multiple priorities"

These phrases feel normal, because we see them so often, but they are loaded.

What's striking is that we already know how to design around this. In everyday life, AI tools now summarise complex documents, translate language, and offer alternative ways to access information without judgement.

We accept these adjustments as sensible, even necessary. Yet in hiring, we still expect candidates to decode vague language, over-specified requirements, and inherited expectations without support.

The irony is that the same technology organisations are racing to adopt for speed and scale could remove barriers at the very first step. Instead, it's often used to automate exclusion more efficiently.

An example of this: I recently reviewed over a hundred live graduate and entry-level job adverts across the UK, spanning the NHS, Civil Service, retail, finance, and tech.

What stood out wasn't variety, but sameness.

Nearly nine in ten demanded "excellent attention to detail" or being "highly organised". Over half emphasised "fast-paced" environments or "working well under pressure". Around a quarter required candidates to be "resilient self-starters".

Almost every advert seemed to say the same thing: "You're not welcome here unless you're flawless".

Here are the numbers:

- **86%** demanded *"excellent attention to detail / highly organised"*
- **58%** pushed *"fast-paced / work well under pressure"*
- **21%** wanted *"sociable / outgoing"*
- **26%** required *"resilient self-starters"*

Now combine these and you start to create profiles of perfection that very rarely exist.

They signal an environment that rewards constant availability, social confidence, tolerance for ambiguity, and energy without recovery. For some candidates, that's appealing; for others, it's a warning sign.

Capable people read these descriptions and opt out; not because they can't do the job, but because they can't see themselves surviving the conditions around it.

Had every opportunity I applied for insisted on "flawless attention to detail", I would never have written an award-winning book; not because I lack ideas or capability, but because my work has always depended on the right scaffolding, support, and systems around me.

That's not a talent shortage.

That's a design failure.

Over-specification and self-exclusion

One of the most consistent patterns I see is this: organisations complain they can't find talent, while simultaneously narrowing the doorway as much as possible.

Excessive experience requirements.

Unnecessary qualifications.

Tool lists that reflect legacy systems rather than actual need.

These requirements often feel reassuring internally. They give the impression of rigour. In practice, they reward confidence over honesty.

I saw this first-hand while working in an organisation recruiting highly specialised roles.

Job descriptions had grown over time to include everything that had ever mattered to anyone involved in the process.

Multiple layers of criteria, duplicated requirements, long explanations designed to satisfy governance, grading frameworks, and risk management, rather than to help a capable person understand what the job actually involved.

Some ran to ten pages or more.

The intention wasn't exclusion; it was reassurance. Each additional requirement felt like it reduced risk.

In reality, it narrowed the field unnecessarily. When we stripped those documents back, removing duplication, simplifying language, and focusing on what genuinely mattered for success; something important happened. The roles didn't change. The job banding didn't change. The standards didn't drop. What changed was accessibility.

Candidates could finally see themselves in the work, rather than getting lost in the paperwork.

That experience reinforced something I now see repeatedly: over-specification doesn't make hiring more robust, it makes it quieter. It filters out people who take requirements seriously, who assume lists are literal, and who opt out rather than over-claim.

The system reads that as a lack of talent; in reality, it's a lack of permission.

People who meet most of the criteria but not all will often still apply if they believe they can "figure it out". Others; particularly neurodivergent candidates, take the list literally and disqualify themselves.

The system doesn't see those people as lost talent. It never sees them at all.

Confidence isn't the same as competence

Hiring processes consistently reward how people present, not how they perform.

Fluent speakers.

Quick thinkers.

People comfortable thinking out loud.

None of these traits are bad. The problem arises when they are mistaken for evidence of capability.

Interviews are artificial environments; they reward certain cognitive styles and penalise others.

When I first started out in recruitment, it was common practice to assess people on their handshake, eye contact, and ability to hold a room in conversation. Those signals were treated as indicators of professionalism and potential.

In reality, they were subjective, poorly evidenced, and exclusionary by design.

People who need time to process, who communicate more precisely than quickly, or who don't perform well under social pressure are often judged as weaker candidates.

Once hired, organisations then complain about performance issues that were never actually tested for.

We keep hiring people who interview well and hoping they will perform well. When they don't, we call it a surprise.

It isn't.

Culture fit and the comfort of sameness

Few phrases do more damage in hiring than "culture fit".

It sounds benign; sensible, even. Who doesn't want people who fit?

The problem is that culture fit is rarely defined. It usually functions as shorthand for familiarity; people who communicate like us, think like us, make us comfortable.

This doesn't mean organisations don't care about values; it means values get conflated with personality.

Difference becomes risk.

Sameness becomes safety.

The result is teams that look aligned but think narrowly.

Innovation slows. Blind spots grow.

The organisation keeps reinforcing its own defaults and wonders why blind spots persist.

Culture should not be about filtering people out; it should be about creating conditions where different contributions can coexist.

In practice, most organisations already contain multiple cultures. Different teams, disciplines, locations, and leadership styles create distinct micro-environments, whether they are acknowledged or not.

The issue isn't their existence; it's whether they are allowed to function openly or are forced to conform to a single, dominant norm.

The strongest organisations recognise this and design for it. They create space for difference to show up without penalty.

That might be through communities of practice, shared interests, identity groups, or side projects; not as add-ons, but as signals of what is genuinely valued.

When culture is treated as something people must fit into, it narrows who gets to belong.

When it's treated as something people help shape, it expands what the organisation is capable of.

Where exclusion really happens

By the time a candidate reaches interview, most of the filtering has already happened..

Which CVs were screened out automatically.

Which ones were skimmed under time pressure.

Which gaps were interpreted as red flags rather than questions.

I'm reminded of this every time I encounter a system that assumes one way of interacting is "normal".

I once went into my local pharmacy in my village to collect a prescription. They asked me to handwrite my name, address, and date of birth on a sticky note.

I started writing, but there was a long queue behind me, and the pressure to be quick made my handwriting messy, as I struggle with handwriting and spelling. The person at the counter looked at it and said loudly, "I can't read this", my stomach sank and my anxiety spiked.

I tried to explain, "I struggle with writing under pressure".

They looked at me blankly. No alternative was offered. No understanding. Just confusion.

It was such a small interaction, but it left me flustered, embarrassed, and exhausted, all before I'd even picked up my prescription.

I could speak the information clearly. I could type it. I could verify it verbally. But the system only recognised one acceptable input. That moment wasn't about capability; it was about a process that prioritised compliance over understanding.

Hiring systems do the same thing. They filter people out not because they lack ability, but because they don't present information in the preferred format.

Technology now accelerates this pattern. Automated screening and AI-driven tools can enforce rigid criteria at speed and scale, amplifying early exclusions rather than questioning them. The format becomes the gatekeeper, regardless of skill.

Recruiters and hiring managers are rarely doing this maliciously. They're responding to incentives: speed over reflection, volume over depth.

The system rewards quick decisions, not thoughtful ones. And because those decisions happen early and invisibly, they're rarely challenged.

What makes this harder is that these patterns are often reproduced under pressure. Someone worried about getting it wrong follows the rule exactly as it's written, even when it causes harm; not because they lack empathy, but because systems reward compliance over judgement.

That's how exclusion persists without intent. The process becomes the authority, and no one feels able to question it.

The cost of hiring this way

When hiring is designed around comfort and familiarity, organisations pay for it later; not immediately, and not always obviously, but consistently.

They pay for it in performance management conversations that feel confusing or circular.

In disengagement that's labelled as attitude rather than exhaustion.

In attrition that's explained away as "not the right fit".

And in repeated hiring cycles that quietly accept churn as inevitable.

Teams then complain about behaviours that were implicitly selected for. Managers struggle with employees who don't adapt to environments that were never designed intentionally in the first place.

Expectations remain unspoken. Support arrives late. Capability is questioned when what's really missing is alignment.

What rarely gets acknowledged is that many of these outcomes were predictable from the moment the role was advertised.

The hiring process rewarded one set of traits and deprioritised others. It filtered for familiarity, then expressed surprise when difference showed up as friction.

This isn't bad luck.

It's the result of systems behaving exactly as they were built to.

A better question to ask

Most hiring processes ask the wrong question.

Not:

"Who feels right?"

Not:

"Who would I enjoy working with?"

But:

"What does this role actually require to succeed, and what conditions allow that success to be sustained?"

We're already seeing this shift emerge, often led by younger generations rather than policy.

The next generation of candidates are far more explicit about flexibility, transparency, and accessibility. They expect clarity around pay, working patterns, and expectations.

In doing so, they're not asking for special treatment; they're normalising conditions many others have had to quietly negotiate or compensate for.

What previous generations had to request as adjustments, the next generation is designing in by default. That should tell us something about where hiring is heading, whether organisations are ready or not.

That shift changes everything.

It moves hiring away from performance theatre and towards capability; away from assumptions and towards design.

Hiring doesn't need to be perfect to be better, but it does need to be intentional.

Until we redesign the front door to work, we will keep wondering why the same people never make it through.

And next, we need to look at what happens when they do.

Designed for Human Action

(Where exclusion starts long before interviews)

This chapter isn't asking you to overhaul hiring; it's asking you to look earlier.

Most hiring systems don't fail randomly; they fail predictably.

Here's the shift worth making.

Stop assuming absence means inability

When someone doesn't apply, the explanation is usually neat and comfortable:

"They weren't right"

"They weren't interested"

"They lacked confidence"

But often, the reality is quieter than that.

They read the advert.

They scanned the requirements.

They picked up on what was being signalled about the environment.

And they made a rational call:

This would cost me too much.

That isn't a motivation issue; it's information.

It's telling you something about the design of the process, the language you're using, and the assumptions baked into how the role is presented.

And even when you think you've got it right, there's another layer people forget.

Candidates who've been through this cycle before; who've applied, adapted, been rejected, and quietly learned the pattern, don't keep trying forever.

They opt out early.

Not because they can't do the job.

But because they recognise the system.

No amount of polished employer branding can compensate for a process that quietly excludes.

People can tell the difference.

Pay attention to what your language is really doing

Look at your last job description; not to improve it, but to understand it.

Ask yourself:

Are we describing the work, or the kind of person we're comfortable with?

Are we outlining tasks, or screening for traits?

Are we signalling support, or perfection?

Job ads don't just describe roles; they set expectations about who will belong before anyone applies.

A reframing worth holding onto

Hiring doesn't fail at interview.

It fails quietly, upstream, by filtering for familiarity instead of capability.

Once you see that, you don't need to change everything.

You just stop being surprised by the outcomes.

Conversation Starter:

"What evidence did we actually see of how this person would do the work; and how much of our decision was based on performance in the interview itself?"

Chapter 5

Interviews reward performance, not ability

Most organisations would like to believe interviews are a fair test; or at least don't want the hassle of managing the alternative!

They feel structured.

They feel objective.

They feel like a sensible way to compare people.

And yet, after the hire is made, the same questions surface again.

"They didn't turn out how we expected"

"They interviewed brilliantly"

"They're struggling in the role"

If interviews were a reliable measure of ability, this wouldn't keep happening.

The uncomfortable truth is that interviews don't test how people do the job; they test how well people perform the interview.

Those two things are not the same.

I've watched this happen, over and over

I've sat in hundreds of interviews: panels, one-to-ones, assessment days, final stages where the decision is supposedly clear.

I've watched confident candidates take up space in the room, speak quickly, fill silences, tell polished stories that land well. I've seen heads nod as people mistake fluency for substance.

I've also watched quieter candidates pause before answering, ask clarifying questions, think carefully, offer precise, thoughtful responses that don't arrive wrapped in confidence.

And I've watched those same candidates get marked down.

Not because they lacked capability, but because they didn't perform in the way the room expected.

Months later, I've seen teams dealing with the consequences: managing underperformance, carrying capability gaps that were never tested properly, wondering how the *"best candidate"* turned out not to be the best hire at all.

This isn't by chance; it follows a pattern you can measure.

Interviews: Artificial Environments that produce Artificial Intelligence

Interviews reward a very specific set of behaviours:

- Thinking out loud under pressure.
- Processing questions quickly.
- Translating experience into neat narratives.
- Managing eye contact, tone, and timing simultaneously.

None of these are core requirements for most roles.

They are, however, skills in their own right, and like any skill, they are unevenly distributed.

For some people, interviews feel energising. For others, they are cognitively expensive. The pressure, the social rules, the expectation to perform confidence on demand; all take a toll.

What's often missed is what happens after someone is hired. We've all seen it: a candidate who matches the role perfectly on paper, with experience in the right systems, organisations, and job titles, yet struggles once inside the role.

Not because they lack capability, but because the way work actually gets done is different. The tools aren't the same. The decision-making norms are unspoken.

"We did it this way there" quietly clashes with "this is how we do things here".

That friction is rarely about skill; it's about misalignment between systems, expectations, and support.

But because the interview rewarded confidence and fluency rather than adaptability and learning, the organisation is surprised when adjustment takes time.

When we treat interviews as normal, we ignore how differently they are experienced and how little they tell us about how someone will navigate a real working environment.

The gap between interview performance and job performance is well established, and yet, despite decades of evidence, we still act surprised when interviews predict the wrong outcomes.

Structured doesn't automatically mean fair

Structured interviews are often presented as the answer to bias; and they do help. They introduce consistency, reduce some forms of subjectivity, and make decision-making easier to justify.

But structure alone doesn't solve the problem.

Most structured interviews still rely on the same underlying demands:

- Verbal recall.
- Linear storytelling.
- Real-time processing.
- Translating experience into abstract examples.

If someone needs time to process, struggles to retrieve examples under pressure, or communicates more precisely than expansively, they are still disadvantaged.

The questions may be standardised, but the cognitive load is not.

What's less often acknowledged is that this pressure doesn't sit solely with the candidate.

Interview panels are made up of humans too. A busy, pressurised hiring manager may be trying to listen carefully, capture accurate notes, score responses in real time, and ensure fairness across candidates; all at once.

Under those conditions, nuance can be lost. Equally, a panel member who excels at seeing the bigger picture but struggles to retain specific details may miss important evidence in the moment.

At the other end of the spectrum, someone who is highly detail-focused may interpret answers very literally, leaving little room for context or alternative ways of demonstrating competence.

None of this reflects intent or professionalism; it reflects how different people process information under pressure.

Structured interviews can reduce chaos.

They can improve consistency.

But they don't automatically measure capability.

This is where organisations often stop short. They improve the mechanics of the process without questioning what the process is actually assessing, or how different people experience it on both sides of the table.

Structure helps.

But it doesn't replace judgement about what actually matters.

When behaviours are misread as ability

I regularly see the same patterns in interviews. Small behaviours get interpreted as indicators of skill when in reality, they often aren't.

Pausing before answering? It's often read as uncertainty.

I remember one candidate who took a few extra seconds to think before responding; even though we'd asked them to take as much time as they needed before responding!

The panel frowned, fidgeted, looked uncomfortable at a brief moment of silence. The candidate just needed to organise their thoughts; something they'd learned over years of high-stakes work, and understanding how to ensure they provided the most relevant response.

But in the interview, that pause was interpreted as doubt.

Asking clarifying questions? Lack of confidence, intellect, or capability.

I once watched someone ask a question to make sure they understood what was being asked. The interviewer looked at the candidate sideways, confused as to why they didn't get the question first time around.

The reality of this situation is that asking clarifying questions is exactly what you want someone to do in a complex role. The behaviour was perfectly competent; the interpretation was wrong.

Giving concise answers? Disengagement or even fabricated experience.

I once saw a candidate give short, precise answers, avoiding long-winded explanations. The panel assumed they weren't interested, or that maybe they didn't have the real experience.

In reality, they were highly skilled and had learned that filler words and repetition don't add value. Conciseness was a strength. But in a system that rewards verbosity, it was read as disengagement.

Even more concerning today, some candidates who communicate directly; clear, concise, to the point, are now flagged as AI-generated. People risk being filtered out simply for speaking like humans who know their stuff.

Not projecting enthusiasm in expected ways? Poor motivation.

I remember a candidate who was calm, quiet, and thoughtful. They didn't jump up in excitement, didn't laugh at every joke, didn't overtly nod or smile.

The panel assumed they weren't motivated. In reality, they were deeply committed; just not in the performative style the panel unconsciously expected. Their motivation was invisible, because the system only "saw" certain expressions.

None of these behaviours reliably predict performance once hired. Yet they shape outcomes because they are filtered through assumptions about what "good" looks like: confidence, extroversion, storytelling style, speed of processing, personality.

Meta-analyses support this: interviewer ratings based on social cues like tone, posture, or expressiveness are weak predictors of actual job performance. When assumptions go unchallenged, interviews reward mirroring the interviewer, not actual capability.

Misread behaviours aren't failures of the candidate; they're the inevitable outcome of systems built around one default way of showing ability.

The false safety of panels

Panel interviews are often treated as a kind of insurance policy: more people in the room, more perspectives, less bias.

That belief is comforting.

It's also only partially true.

Research does show that **structured interviews**, including structured panels, are more predictive than unstructured, conversational ones. When everyone is asked the same questions, in the same order, with clear criteria, outcomes improve. Bias is reduced. Accuracy goes up; not dramatically, but meaningfully.

The problem is that this isn't how most panels actually operate.

What organisations *say* they're running is a structured panel; what they're often running is a group conversation with a score sheet.

In those conditions, panels aren't especially accurate. Predictive validity for typical, loosely structured interviews remains low to moderate at best; better than a coin toss, yes, but nowhere near the gold standard, which we already know involves combining structured interviews with work samples and evidence of real capability.

And panels come with costs we rarely acknowledge.

They increase pressure.

They raise the cognitive load.

They reward candidates who can perform under social strain rather than those who will do the job well once the strain is removed.

Multiple interviewers mean multiple signals to read: who's nodding, who's sceptical, who matters most. For some candidates, that's manageable. For others, it's overwhelming, and entirely unrelated to how they'll perform in role.

Panels also introduce a quieter risk: **groupthink**.

Adding more people doesn't automatically add more independent judgement; especially when panel members share similar backgrounds, sit in the same hierarchy, or come from the same function. In those rooms, early confidence carries disproportionate weight. A senior voice anchors the discussion. Scores drift towards agreement. What looks like rigour is often just alignment.

I've been invited onto panels specifically to interrupt that dynamic; not to override decisions, but to challenge the certainty around them, to ask why one candidate feels "safe" and another feels "risky".

To uncover when feelings of doubt are being read as facts.

Even when I was outvoted, two to one, with both other panellists from the same department, the real impact often came later; in reflection, when outcomes didn't match expectations, when the next panel moved more carefully, having recognised how quickly consensus formed last time.

This is where AI creates a real fork in the road.

Used badly, it will make panels more dangerous: cleaner summaries, faster scoring, stronger justifications for decisions that were never very robust to begin with.

Used well, it can make panels more honest.

When notes are captured automatically, interviewers can stop performing attentiveness and actually listen. When evidence is recorded clearly, it becomes harder to hide behind vague discomfort or "gut feel". When roles are explicit, who probes, who observes, who challenges, it's easier to see influence, hierarchy, and bias in real time.

Panels don't fail because people are malicious or careless; they fail because they offer the *appearance* of objectivity while quietly rewarding conformity.

If we use AI to polish that appearance, we won't improve hiring.

We'll simply professionalise our confidence in decisions that were never as solid as we thought.

Performance theatre versus real work

Interviews often reward a narrow kind of performance.

That doesn't make them useless, but it does mean we need to be honest about what they show us.

They show us how someone performs in a highly artificial, time-limited, socially loaded situation.

Most interviews also restrict how candidates are allowed to demonstrate what they know. Experience must be spoken, recalled on demand, and translated into neat examples within a narrow time window.

There are rarely alternative routes to evidence capability; no opportunity to show how someone thinks over time, how they work with information, or how they approach real problems once the pressure is removed.

When the only way to demonstrate your skills is through a single, rigid format, so much of what someone can actually do goes unseen. Capability that doesn't express itself fluently under interview conditions is discounted; not because it's absent, but because the process has no way to recognise it.

This is not a flaw in the candidate; it's a limitation of the assessment.

They do not show us how someone thinks when given space.

They do not show us how someone solves problems over time.

They do not show us how someone contributes once the pressure is removed.

One organisation I worked with recognised this problem and decided to experiment with **walking interviews**.

For roles where most of the work is done on your feet; moving around the building, supporting people, responding to situations as they happen, sitting in a windowless room being asked questions about that work just didn't make sense.

So they gave candidates a choice: take the traditional interview, or walk through the environment where they'd actually be working.

And the difference was immediate.

Being in the kitchen, the workshop, or the care area, candidates could see the space, the equipment, the potential hazards, the people they'd interact with.

Even if they hadn't experienced a particular scenario recently, they could imagine what it would be like and explain how they'd respond. Visual, tactile, real-world context sparked ideas and allowed them to demonstrate thinking, problem-solving, and decision-making in ways a chair-and-table interview never could.

It was a simple shift, but it changed the performance entirely. Candidates weren't asked to perform theatre anymore; they were asked to show what they could do in the environment where the work actually happens. And by making it a choice, the organisation respected individual comfort while unlocking a richer, more accurate view of capability.

When assessment looks nothing like the job, it shouldn't surprise us when it predicts the wrong outcomes.

Walking interviews are one example of designing a process that meets candidates where they are, and finally lets them show what they're capable of in a way that actually matters.

A system problem, not a people problem

Most interview bias isn't malicious; it's inherited.

Processes get reused.

Questions get copied.

Formats persist because they feel familiar, or because they feel defensible.

I once worked with a team where every hiring manager was using the same interview questions that had been in the handbook for a decade.

Nobody remembered why those questions were there, and nobody had tested whether they actually revealed the skills the role required. Candidates who struggled with those questions looked "less capable", even if they'd have excelled on the job. Over time, that single, unquestioned approach quietly shaped who got noticed, and who didn't.

Changing them seemed a bigger task than it was, so nobody wanted to take it on, and so nothing changed.

When we rely on methods that reward confidence, speed, and performance under pressure, we reliably select for those traits; and then act surprised when people who excelled in the interview, struggle in the real role, which demands something different.

The fault isn't with the candidate; it's with what we chose to value, and how we chose to measure it.

When feedback causes harm

Interview feedback is rarely treated as something that can damage health or confidence.

But it can, and often does.

Poor feedback doesn't just disappoint candidates.

It undermines confidence.

It erodes trust in the employer.

And it quietly damages the credibility of the person delivering it.

What's striking is how rarely organisations recognise this.

Candidates aren't naïve; they recognise vague, tokenistic feedback instantly.

"Not quite the right fit"

"Strong candidate, but..."

"We went in another direction"

These phrases don't protect people; they confuse them.

The issue isn't intent. Most managers aren't trying to be careless or cruel; they're acting within a system that tells them to *give feedback*, but also to *protect themselves*.

So feedback becomes defensive: carefully worded, non-committal, safe.

And in becoming safe for the organisation, it becomes useless, and sometimes actively harmful, for the human on the receiving end.

This is what happens when systems are designed without considering modern human consequences.

And here's the uncomfortable truth: if we don't confront this now, we will automate it.

AI won't fix vague feedback.

It will scale it; faster, cheaper, and at volume.

That's why this isn't a feedback issue; it's how the work has been set up.

And even when feedback isn't actively harmful, the hiring

process itself often quietly fails people. That's where we start seeing the tangible costs of getting it wrong.

The real cost of getting it wrong

Until organisations are willing to redesign interviews around real work, they will keep hiring the same problems and wondering why nothing changes.

We are hiring for the interview, then blaming the hire.

And the consequences don't stop with the person who gets the job.

Far more candidates are rejected than accepted. For most people, the interview system ends not with an offer, but with an experience; and that experience stays with them.

There have been well-documented cases where poor candidate experience has had a direct commercial impact.

One of the most widely cited examples comes from Virgin Media, who discovered they were losing millions in revenue due to poor candidate experience during interviews.

Rejected candidates were going home, cancelling their services, and switching to competitors.

The organisation responded by overhauling its recruitment experience; not as a branding exercise, but because the cost of getting it wrong was measurable.

That's the macro picture.

At the micro level, the same damage happens quietly, every day.

Designed for Human Action

(Where assessment mistakes confidence for competence)

This chapter isn't arguing that interviews are useless; it's asking you to be honest about what they actually measure.

Here's how to accept that responsibility, without blowing things up.

What we tend to reward without noticing

Pay attention to what impresses you in interviews:

Speed of thought, fluency, confidence under pressure.

None of these are inherently bad.

But none of them reliably predict performance either.

When they dominate decisions, you're not selecting for ability; you're selecting for comfort.

And comfort has a style.

What to question after the decision feels "obvious"

Instead of asking:

"Who came across best?"

Try asking:

"What evidence did we actually see of how this person would do the work?"

If the answer is mostly conversational, hypothetical, or performance-based, that isn't a failure of judgement; it's a signal about the design of the assessment.

A line worth holding onto

If your assessment looks nothing like the job,

don't be surprised when it predicts the wrong outcomes.

That isn't a hiring problem.

It's a design choice.

And design choices, inherited, unquestioned, or outdated; still produce outcomes.

If you didn't design the interview, the criteria, or the process yourself,

you're still responsible for what it selects for.

Ownership doesn't mean starting again.

It means noticing what your system is actually rewarding, and deciding whether that's what you intend.

Conversation Starter:

"What's one thing you wish someone had told you in your first month here?"

Chapter 6

Onboarding: where good intent quietly unravels

Most organisations think of onboarding as administrative.

Logins. Policies. Inductions. A few meetings in the diary. Maybe a welcome lunch if someone remembers.

It's treated as something to get through, rather than as something that shapes how people experience work from that point on.

And yet, onboarding is one of the most influential systems an organisation has; not because it teaches people how to do their job, but because it teaches them what kind of place they've joined.

Onboarding as a trust signal

I've learned to see onboarding as a trust signal.

Not a process, not a checklist, but a signal.

I live in a village, and not long ago I watched a story unfold locally on the news that has stayed with me.

So much so, I ended up interviewing a teacher from a school and a local authority representative responsible for supporting young people into work straight from specialist education settings.

They shared the story of the young man who was in the news with his family; who is non-verbal and autistic, and how he entered employment through a supported pathway that didn't rely on talk, guesswork, or "just watch how others do it".

Before he joined the company he works for, there was hesitation within the team; quiet uncertainty, people wondering how someone who is non-verbal would manage day to day.

How communication would work. Whether it would slow others down. These weren't unkind thoughts; they were assumptions, formed without experience.

Instead of leaving those assumptions to play out, the role was designed differently from the start. Tasks were broken down visually. Expectations were explicit. Support was front-loaded, not drip-fed after mistakes. Communication worked on his terms, using pre-defined word cards and shared cues rather than inference.

Within a relatively short period of time, the tone of the conversation had shifted completely.

Team members spoke about reliability. About clarity. About trust. They described him as one of the most productive people in the team; someone they could rely on to deliver. He wasn't managed more closely than others. He was trusted, because the work had been made clear enough to earn that trust.

Independent.

Productive.

Part of the team.

The difference wasn't his capability, it was how he was onboarded.

That's why onboarding matters more than most organisations realise. When it's designed with difference in mind, rather than treated as an exception to be managed later, people don't spend their first weeks decoding hidden rules or masking uncertainty. They learn early that it's safe to ask or raise a hand, safe to need clarity, and safe to be human.

Get that signal right and confidence, performance, and belonging follow quickly. Get it wrong, and people adapt silently; often at a cost that only becomes visible much later.

In the first few weeks, people are paying close attention; not looking for perfection, but for consistency. They're watching to see whether what was promised in the interview actually exists once they arrive. They're testing whether it's safe to ask questions, admit uncertainty, or slow down long enough to learn.

Most people don't decide whether they belong six months in; they decide far earlier, often before anyone notices.

When information is scattered, expectations are vague, and support is reactive rather than intentional, people learn quickly that they're expected to figure things out alone.

People who've faced systemic barriers previously tend to read that signal faster, because the cost of getting it wrong is higher.

And when onboarding fails, people rarely push back. They adapt. They mask. They overcompensate. Once that pattern is set, it's very hard to undo.

This is where goodwill quietly drains away.

Cognitive overload isn't just about volume

Many organisations treat the first 30 days as a probationary warm-up; a period to absorb information, find your feet, and start contributing gradually.

The assumption is that uncertainty decreases naturally over time, as people "settle in" and confidence grows.

In reality, uncertainty accumulates.

Unclear expectations, unspoken norms, and inconsistent guidance don't fade away.

They stack.

Each small moment of confusion becomes another decision to second-guess, another question not asked, another workaround quietly built.

For some people, this early ambiguity is cognitively expensive. Instead of focusing on learning the role, energy is spent decoding the environment.

When onboarding relies on time to fix what should have been designed upfront, uncertainty doesn't resolve itself; it becomes the backdrop to how work is experienced from that point on.

Onboarding is often described as overwhelming because there's "too much information".

That's only part of the problem.

Cognitive overload isn't simply about how much there is to process;

It's about ambiguity, unclear expectations, unspoken rules, and moving targets.

Most organisations imagine the first 30 days as orientation:

accounts set up, paperwork completed, introductions made.

By the end of the month, the assumption is that people are "settling in".

Cognitively, something very different is happening.

New starters are working out what actually matters and what doesn't:

Which questions are safe to ask.

How quickly they're expected to respond.

What mistakes are tolerated, and which ones quietly count against them.

For people who don't instinctively pick up unspoken rules, this isn't background noise;

it's work.

Not knowing what's expected.

Not knowing who to ask.

Not knowing whether asking will be seen as a lack of competence.

That uncertainty drains energy long before any meaningful contribution begins. Time is spent second-guessing, rehearsing questions, replaying interactions and trying not to be seen as difficult or slow.

From the outside, this looks like someone taking time to settle in; from the inside, it feels like running with a weight you were never told you'd be carrying.

People who have learned, often through experience, that getting things wrong comes with disproportionate consequences tend to feel that weight earlier and more intensely.

They observe more closely, they adapt faster, they mask sooner, and they work harder, earlier, simply to stay safe.

The unspoken rules no one explains

Most onboarding programmes focus on what people need to know.

Very few focus on what people need to understand:

How decisions are really made.

How visible you're expected to be.

Whether it's acceptable to challenge, or safer to comply.

What "good enough" actually looks like here.

These things are rarely written down. They're absorbed socially. Through observation, inference, and correction.

I've seen this show up in small, ordinary moments:

Someone three weeks in, still unsure whether they're meant to speak in meetings or wait to be invited.

Over-preparing for everything because expectations haven't been made explicit. Rewriting messages repeatedly, trying to get the tone right.

People still not even being sure where the kitchen is, or how to get to a specific department, but dare not ask again!

Nothing dramatic. Nothing that triggers concern.

Just quiet effort going into surviving the system, rather than doing the job.

"Ask if you need anything" doesn't work

One of the most common onboarding phrases is also one of the least effective.

"Just ask if you need anything"

The people most affected by unclear systems are often the least likely to feel safe pointing them out.

On the surface, the phrase sounds supportive. In practice, it shifts responsibility onto the person with the least context, the least confidence in the environment, and the least power in the system.

To ask for help, someone needs to know what they don't yet know. They need to know who to ask. And they need to trust that asking won't quietly change how they're perceived.

That trust doesn't exist by default; especially for people who have learned, through experience, that being visible can come with a cost, that asking questions can be read as weakness, that getting it wrong early can stick.

So they don't ask.

They watch.

They guess.

They compensate.

Those early patterns don't just shape confidence; they quietly set the ceiling for performance.

Onboarding creates management problems later

Poor onboarding doesn't just affect the person joining; it creates problems that managers inherit months or even years down the line.

I've seen it play out the same way in team after team:

Someone starts in a role, told to figure out a system or process on their own. They cobble it together, do just enough to get by, and mask the parts they don't fully understand. Six months later, gaps start to show. The manager notices, gives guidance, but because the employee "should already know it", they rarely get real training. They cobble along again, and things seem fine... until a few months later, under pressure, the same issues resurface.

And then it happens again. And again.

Sometimes this cycle repeats for years. I've seen people with twenty years of experience in an organisation still caught in it; competent, skilled, and once motivated, but constantly tripped up by systems, processes, or technology that were never properly taught. It's not a performance issue; it's a design failure from the very start.

The impact isn't just on the individual; managers are constantly firefighting, trying to fix gaps they didn't create, while teams experience repeated disruptions.

One small onboarding oversight becomes a long-term, systemic problem that hits multiple systems, creates chronic friction, and quietly erodes trust in leadership.

This is just one example; there are countless others. The problem rarely lies with capability or motivation. It's almost always about a system, a process, or a tool that wasn't designed or supported properly.

And until organisations tackle that root cause, the cycle continues.

Energy, not time

When energy is spent early on survival, it's no longer available later for learning, growth, or resilience.

By the time organisations notice performance issues, the cost has already been paid.

It just doesn't show up on a timeline.

Onboarding is often treated as a time-based problem:

Give people a few weeks.

Let them settle.

Trust that things will improve.

But time doesn't replenish energy. Systems decide whether it's drained or protected.

That's why early onboarding strain isn't about effort or attitude, but about how uncertainty drains energy in predictable ways, and why that cost sits with the system, not the individual.

What we call "energy" at work isn't motivation; it's attention, emotional regulation, and the capacity to absorb new information under uncertainty.

It's finite. And it's easiest to drain when everything is new, unclear, and exposed.

When systems are ambiguous, people burn energy just to stay afloat:

Decoding expectations.

Second-guessing what "good" looks like.

Managing how they're perceived.

Trying not to stand out for the wrong reasons.

The effort it takes is almost invisible, but it has real consequences. Stress narrows attention. It reduces learning. It makes mistakes more likely, not less. By the time people are expected to perform, much of their usable energy has already been spent.

From the outside, it can look like someone "not quite getting there yet".

From the inside, it feels like starting every day slightly depleted.

Good onboarding doesn't rush people; it removes friction early, so energy can go into contribution rather than self-protection.

And when organisations get this wrong, the impact isn't just slower ramp-up; it's higher attrition, more errors, quieter disengagement, and a workforce that never quite recovers the capacity it lost in the first few weeks.

Designed onboarding versus accidental onboarding

Accidental onboarding relies on goodwill, confidence, and social fluency.

Designed onboarding recognises that not everyone enters the organisation with the same internal resources.

It doesn't reduce standards; it makes them clearer.

It doesn't over-explain; it makes the important things explicit.

It doesn't single people out; it builds structure that works for most people.

When onboarding is designed with humans in mind, people don't have to guess how to belong; they're shown.

And when that happens, performance issues reduce, trust builds earlier, and managers inherit people who are ready to contribute rather than recover.

But onboarding is only the first system people encounter.

After that, everything depends on how they're managed.

That's where things either start to work, or quietly fall apart again.

Designed for Human Action

(How to reduce early friction by making expectations visible)

Onboarding is where good intent often unravels.

Most organisations think of it as logistics:

Paperwork, systems, introductions.

But for the person joining, especially a neurodivergent one, onboarding is where they decide something much more fundamental:

Is this place safe?

Is it predictable?

And is it worth the energy it's going to take to stay?

When people struggle early, disengage quietly, or burn energy before they've even started contributing, it's rarely because they're not capable; it's because too much is left unsaid.

If this chapter felt familiar, here's where to begin.

Start by questioning what you've learned to accept.

There are a few phrases that come up again and again when onboarding doesn't quite work:

"They'll find their feet"

"They just need time"

"It's always overwhelming at first"

When new starters keep getting caught out in the same ways, asking the same questions, pausing at the same points, missing the same unspoken rules, that isn't part of "settling in";

It's the system showing you where it's failing.

And if the pattern repeats, the problem isn't people's resilience;

It's what hasn't been made clear.

Then, stop trying to toughen people up.

Don't make the first month a test of endurance.

Redesign what people are expected to navigate instead.

Focus on the first 30 days, not the whole journey.

Because how people learn to survive in month one often shapes how they show up for years.

Ask yourself:

- What decisions are people making before they understand how things really work?

- What information arrives only after it would have been useful?
- What are we assuming people will "pick up" just by watching others?

Better onboarding doesn't mean more content; it means better sequencing.

The right information, at the right time, in a format people can actually use.

Make the invisible rules visible.

Most onboarding fails not because people aren't told enough, but because the *important things* are never named.

Be explicit about:

- What success looks like in the first few weeks
- What *not* to worry about yet
- Who to go to for what, and when
- How feedback really works here
- What "good enough" looks like before confidence shows up

If someone has to infer how to belong, the system is doing too much work in their head.

And that comes at a cost.

Clarity reduces anxiety.

Anxiety drains energy.

And drained energy kills performance before it's even had a chance to show up.

Try a few shifts without waiting for permission.

You don't need a new onboarding programme to do this better.

You can:

- Break the first month into named phases
- Share written context before meetings
- Be clear about what matters now, and what can wait
- Show examples of good work early
- Ask "what helps you settle in?" and show some examples of what's previously helped others, instead of "any questions?"

These aren't adjustments for a few people.

They're accelerators for most people.

If something helps someone contribute sooner, it's not indulgent.

It's better communication.

One question to carry forward

Before you move on, think on this:

"If someone struggled in their first month here, would we see that as feedback on them, or on us?"

Because onboarding doesn't just introduce people to the role; it teaches them how much effort survival will require.

And once that lesson is learned, it's very hard to unlearn.

Conversation Starter:

"What's one thing you wish someone had told you in your first month here?"

One Small Experiment

Ask a human question

This week, ask a new starter or a recent hire:

"What's one thing about our onboarding that confused you or made you feel like an outsider?"

Notice what comes up, and what doesn't. You don't need to fix it yet; just listen.

Chapter 7

Managing difference without patronising people

Policies matter. Frameworks matter. Culture decks matter.

But day to day, inclusion lives or dies in one place: the relationship between a manager and the people they manage.

I've come to see this as one of the biggest misunderstandings in modern organisations. We talk about inclusion as though it lives in strategy, values, or policy.

Policy shapes intention. Management shapes experience.

When something starts to go wrong for someone who works differently, it rarely shows up as a dramatic failure. It shows up quietly: energy drops, questions stop, confidence erodes, output might still look fine, for a while.

From the organisation's point of view, nothing appears broken.

From the individual's point of view, everything has become harder.

This is how systems fail; not through bad intent, but through a slow burnout. The further responsibility sits from day-to-day work, the more pressure lands on the person closest to it. And that person is almost always the manager.

Whether leaders acknowledge it or not, managers are where systems become real.

For people whose best work depends on clarity, trust, and mutual understanding, that relationship often determines whether work becomes sustainable or slowly unbearable.

Not because managers are unkind, but because many have been set up to fail by systems that quietly avoid responsibility.

Like many people, I've had experiences where I was managed by someone and everything worked. We found a way. There was mutual understanding. Expectations were clear enough. Adjustments happened without drama.

Then the manager changed; sometimes through promotion, sometimes because someone left, sometimes because of a reorganisation. No blame. Just the normal evolution of organisations.

This has happened to me several times. And yes, systems and processes often shift alongside it. But it's the change in manager that has the biggest impact.

Suddenly, the person managing you isn't familiar with how you work. They bring their own assumptions, preferences, and ways of operating.

What was once understood now needs explaining. What was once accommodated becomes questioned. Their way of working collides with yours.

What really changes here is tolerance.

A new manager arrives without context. They haven't seen how someone thinks, how they recover, or what conditions make their best work possible. What was once understood gets reinterpreted. What was once allowed quietly becomes something that needs justification.

Support that once happened naturally now needs explaining. And because it was never built into the system, it disappears the moment the relationship changes.

It shouldn't rely this heavily on individual relationships; it demonstrates how much of work still depends on individual goodwill rather than shared understanding.

What was once a comfortable, enjoyable role can become stressful almost overnight. Conversations feel more effortful. Feedback feels sharper. The work starts to feel combative rather than collaborative.

It shouldn't be this way.

And yet, I hear this same story played out in organisations across the world.

The discomfort nobody names

Most managers want to do the right thing. That matters.

But when difference shows up at work, it often brings a discomfort that rarely gets acknowledged.

Managers worry about:

- Saying the wrong thing.
- Being accused of favouritism.
- Lowering standards.
- Opening a conversation they don't know how to close.

So they do what humans often do when they're unsure: they avoid.

Avoid the conversation.

Avoid clarity.

Avoid naming difference at all.

On the surface, this can look calm. Sensible. Even professional.

Don't make a fuss.

Don't single anyone out.

Keep things "fair".

From the inside, it feels very different.

It feels like no one has your back.

When organisations stay quiet, the questions don't disappear; they just move inward.

People start guessing what's expected.

Masking what feels risky.

Carrying the uncertainty themselves.

And that quiet, unspoken effort becomes part of the job, even though it was never meant to be.

Why managers default to avoidance

Managers are too often asked to carry complexity without being given tools.

They're told to "be inclusive" but not shown how.

They're encouraged to support difference but warned not to get it wrong.

They're expected to manage performance while simultaneously managing wellbeing, with little guidance on how those two actually interact.

So they fall back on what feels safest.

Time-based measures.

Visibility.

Responsiveness.

Behavioural cues that feel objective because they're familiar.

Those cues tend to disadvantage people who don't work in standard ways. The impact is often felt earliest and most sharply by neurodivergent employees, but the pattern itself is broader than that.

I hear some version of this hesitation in almost every leadership conversation I'm invited into. Managers aren't resistant to inclusion; they're anxious about getting it wrong.

And anxiety rarely produces good results; it produces silence.

That silence is often mistaken for doing nothing.

But for the person on the receiving end, it feels like absence.

Not hostility.

Not cruelty.

Just a quiet withdrawal of support.

Adjustments are not indulgence

One of the most persistent myths in teams, and from the perspective of managers, is that adjustments are a form of leniency.

A personal gift.

Something quietly handed to one individual, which they should be eternally grateful for; and sometimes subtly guilt-ridden about.

As if they've been given food while the rest of the team are left hungry.

That framing creates exactly what managers say they want to avoid: othering, resentment, and rivalry between people who are meant to be working together.

Adjustments aren't indulgences.

And they're not a "golden handshake" either.

They are simply a way of removing friction that never needed to be there in the first place.

They exist to help someone meet expectations, not escape them.

What causes resentment isn't adjustments themselves; it's when adjustments are invisible, poorly explained, or applied inconsistently.

When managers frame adjustments as *part of how work gets done*, rather than as a favour to an individual, the temperature drops almost immediately.

Yes, there will always be people who take advantage.

But when we respond by putting barriers in place to make everyone *look* equal, we actively dismantle equity.

Because we are not designed the same way.

And we have not all had equal opportunities to be our best selves.

Supporting people differently isn't unfair; it's intentional.

And when we give people the tools and adaptations they need to succeed *as individuals*, the team gets stronger, not weaker.

The clarity managers underestimate

People don't want wrapping in cotton wool.

They want things to be clear.

They want to know:

- What matters most this week.
- What can wait.
- How their work will be judged.
- When something is good enough.

Ambiguity is often more stressful than feedback.

Yet managers frequently soften messages in the name of kindness, leaving people to infer meaning instead. This is where misunderstandings multiply.

Being direct is not the same as being harsh.

Being explicit is not the same as being controlling.

In fact, clarity is one of the most supportive things a manager can offer.

I've seen people thrive not because pressure was reduced, but because uncertainty was. When expectations are explicit, energy goes into the work instead of into decoding the environment.

Being clear doesn't make work easier; it just removes the unnecessary noise.

And noise is one of the biggest drains on sustainable performance.

When being clear to your people is avoided, issues don't disappear. They surface later, reframed as performance problems or formal disputes, long after the opportunity to support someone properly has passed.

That outcome helps no one.

Performance conversations that don't cause harm

Many managers worry that acknowledging neurodivergence will undermine performance conversations.

The opposite is usually true.

When difference is named safely, performance becomes easier to talk about. Expectations can be adjusted without being diluted. Feedback can be grounded in outcomes rather than behaviours.

The key shift is this:

talk about the work, not the person.

Instead of:

"You need to be more proactive"

Try:

"This role needs earlier visibility of risks. Let's agree how that shows up in practice"

That isn't softer. It's clearer.

You can then look at what systems, tools, and potentially adjustments can help support the successful delivery of the work.

Behaviour is often treated as a personal trait, when it's more accurately a response to context. When the environment changes, behaviour often does too.

Performance conversations that ignore context tend to personalise problems that were never personal in the first place. When managers shift the focus back to outcomes and conditions, those conversations become both firmer and fairer.

That's often what makes the difference between someone staying on track and someone slowly coming of the rails.

Disclosure shouldn't live in the moment; it's a process

One of the most fragile points in the manager relationship is disclosure.

Too often it's treated as a one-off event; a box ticked exercise, or a conversation had.

In reality, disclosure evolves. What someone needs in their first six months may not be what they need two years in. Energy changes. Roles change. Context changes.

Life changes!

I've seen people disclose once, get support for a while, and then slowly stop asking as their role changed; not because their needs disappeared, but because the conversation never reopened.

I've also seen managers do everything "right" at disclosure, then unknowingly punish honesty later by treating future requests as inconvenience rather than context.

The regret doesn't usually come at disclosure. It comes six months later, when the volume on support gets quietly turned down.

This is why disclosure is better understood as

maintenance, not permission. Support needs checking in on, not signed off.

The risk isn't that people ask for too much; it's that they stop asking altogether. When that happens, organisations often mistake silence for a happy and content employee, right up until the cost shows up somewhere else.

Good managers don't treat disclosure as static information; they treat it as an ongoing dialogue.

And crucially, they don't make people regret being honest.

Disclosure is often treated like a piece of information being handed over:

- A diagnosis.
- A profile.
- A note on a file.
- A conversation recorded and then quietly "completed".

That disclosure might be about a parent who is receiving end of life care. It might be about an employees ADHD or autism. It might be physical, neurological, or emotional ill health. It might be about being a parent to a disabled child.

Some disclosures are temporary. Some are lifelong. All of them carry weight.

But information on its own doesn't create understanding.

In fact, without context, it can do the opposite.

Managers are sometimes given just enough information to feel cautious, but not enough to be genuinely helpful. And when that happens, support quietly turns into risk management.

Someone becomes:

- A potential HR case
- A sensitivity issue
- A "special situation"

Not because anyone is trying to be unkind.

But because uncertainty makes people retreat to what feels safe.

And in organisations, safety often looks like reducing opportunity rather than opening it up:

- Less stretch work
- Less ambiguity
- Less visibility
- More control, framed as support

It's often meant as protection, but it ends up limiting people instead.

That's why the most useful response to disclosure isn't a file note or a one-off conversation. It's something more ordinary, and more human. An ongoing dialogue about how work is experienced, rather than what someone is labelled.

What helps you do your best work here?

What reliably gets in the way?

What support still makes sense, and what no longer does?

Information should widen possibility, not shrink it.

When that happens, the system starts working against the very people it's meant to support.

When managers become the buffer

Good managers quietly absorb system failures, so individuals don't have to.

They translate vague strategy into concrete priorities.

They shield people from unnecessary noise.

They push back on expectations that look reasonable on paper but collapse in practice.

They also know how policy actually works.

Not as a rigid rulebook, but as something to be interpreted with judgement. They understand where there is room to flex, where discretion is allowed, and when it's appropriate to challenge process in order to support someone doing their job well.

That isn't weakness.

It's leadership.

Well-onboarded managers, who understand the culture as well as the rules, tend to do this instinctively. They know which battles matter. They know when following the letter of a process will create more harm than benefit. And they have the confidence to ask questions, escalate thoughtfully, or quietly adapt when something clearly isn't working.

This kind of leadership rarely gets recognised, because it doesn't announce itself. It shows up as fewer escalations, quieter teams, and problems that never quite materialise.

But it's not invisible to the people experiencing it. For them, it's often the difference between coping and contributing.

This is also why change of manager can be so destabilising. When a new manager joins an organisation, they often don't yet know the informal rules, the history, or where flexibility exists. Without that context, they default to process. Policies get applied more rigidly.

Discretion disappears. Support that once felt human starts to feel conditional.

Nothing has officially changed.

But the buffer is gone.

On my podcast, *Neurodiversity with Theo Smith*, I've spoken to a lot of brilliant managers. The ones who stand out aren't the loud, shiny "leadership" types. They're the people who quietly make work survivable. They don't just manage tasks, they translate the environment.

One story that's stayed with me came from two guests I met at an event: **Mima** and **John**.

Mima is a Lego-obsessed forester. Trees, maps, apps, cricket; her dream job in real life. John is her manager. Outdoorsy, practical, curious, and refreshingly honest about what he didn't know at the start.

On paper, Mima looked like the kind of candidate everyone says they want: first-class degree, confident speaker, visible talent. John had even seen her speak and thought, *I just want to meet her. She's fascinating.*

But there was a barrier that would have quietly shut a lot of doors: Mima had started having seizures at university, and she couldn't drive. In forestry, that matters. John could have made that the end of the conversation.

Instead, he offered her the placement and decided they'd find a way to make it work.

Then she started the job… and it was rough.

Not because she couldn't do the work; she could, and in some areas she was brilliant. But the *experience* of work hit hard. The routine. The constant social processing. The unspoken expectations. The pressure to look capable. She was masking constantly, trying to appear "fine", then going home completely empty. Early nights. No energy. Meltdowns. More seizures.

And there were tasks that seemed simple to everyone else but weren't simple to her at all. Measuring timber stacks, for example: John could eyeball it. Mima needed a tape measure. She was slow, unsure, and getting more stressed by the minute; not because she was lazy or incompetent, but because her brain didn't process that kind of spatial judgement in the same automatic way.

From John's side, it was confusing. He'd hired this inspiring, articulate person and now he was watching her become exhausted within weeks. He didn't know what was going on, but he knew something wasn't right.

Here's where the "manager as buffer" really begins.

John went away and got curious. He spoke to his wife, who works in early years, and she asked a question that shifted everything: "Do you think she might be autistic?"

John admits he had stereotypes in his head; most people do. But instead of dismissing it, he started reading, connecting dots, and slowly seeing a pattern that explained what both of them were struggling to name.

Eventually he raised it with Mima, carefully, awkwardly, humanly, and asked if she'd ever considered autism.

Mima's response was wonderfully Mima: calm, deadpan, almost casual. Not a big emotional moment. Just: *oh, okay*. But what changed wasn't a label, it was the relationship.

They made one agreement that opened the door to everything else: Mima could ask questions. About anything. Without judgement.

And once that permission was real, the pressure started to lift. They began translating the workplace together; not just tasks, but language, expectations, unspoken rules. They built small, practical supports that made the day doable: recognising early signs of overload, taking breaks before meltdown, changing the physical environment when needed, reducing unnecessary stressors, sorting food and routines so basic needs didn't collapse under pressure.

None of it was dramatic. It was just good management: noticing friction, removing what didn't need to be hard, and helping someone do great work without constantly paying for it in exhaustion.

The outcome was powerful.

Mima stabilised. Her confidence returned. The work became sustainable. And John said something that matters: the process didn't just support Mima, it changed him too. It made him reflect on his own assumptions, his own habits, his own version of masking.

That's the bit I want leaders to understand.

When managers become the buffer, it isn't "special treatment", It's what good leadership looks like in the real world: creating the conditions where someone can contribute, not just cope.

Neuroinclusive management isn't about knowing everything, or bending rules indiscriminately. It's about noticing when systems are getting in the way of good work, and being willing to adjust the environment rather than placing all the responsibility on the individual.

That willingness is what makes work sustainable, for everyone.

What this chapter is really asking of managers

Not that they get it right every time.

Not that they have the perfect response.

Not that they become experts overnight.

What matters more is whether they stay present:

Present in conversations that don't have neat answers.

Present when someone is still delivering, but clearly carrying more than they should.

Present enough to notice when the system is making work harder than it needs to be.

Because, in practice, managers are the system that people experience day to day.

And when that presence is there, inclusion stops feeling abstract and starts showing up in the small, ordinary moments that actually matter.

Designed for Human Action

(How to support difference without asking managers to improvise)

If you're a manager reading this, this next part isn't a demand on you, it's a design challenge for the organisation around you.

Managers don't set out to exclude people.

Most of the time, they're trying to keep work moving, hit targets, and avoid getting it wrong.

What they're often being asked to do, though, is compensate for systems that were never designed to support difference in the first place.

Inclusion lives or dies in the gap between expectation and reality.

And that gap is where managers are left to improvise.

If this chapter feels familiar, here's where to start.

Start by noticing what managers are quietly carrying.

There are a few things I hear again and again in training rooms and Q&A sessions after keynotes:

"I don't know what to say"

"I'm worried I'll get it wrong"

"I don't want to treat them differently"

When managers get stuck here, they often freeze; not because they don't care, but because they don't feel equipped to act.

Without language, permission, or structure, doing nothing can feel safer than doing the wrong thing.

But avoidance isn't the safest bet; it quietly transfers the cost onto the employee.

. . .

Next, stop asking managers to be something they're not.

Don't try to train managers to be therapists.

That's not the job.

Redesign the expectations of the role instead.

Whether you manage people directly, or influence how management is set up, these are worth asking:

- What decisions are managers expected to make without guidance?
- Where are they relying on instinct instead of clarity?
- Which support conversations are framed as "nice to have" rather than core to the role?

Managing people isn't a soft skill layered on top of delivery; it *is* the delivery system.

If expectations are vague, outcomes will be inconsistent, no matter how well-intentioned the manager.

Then, make the lines clearer than they currently are.

Managers struggle most when the rules are implicit.

Be explicit about things that are currently left to guesswork:

- What "good performance" actually means beyond output
- How flexibility can show up without lowering standards
- What managers are responsible for; and what they're not
- How adjustment conversations can happen without waiting for formal disclosure

When managers don't know where the lines are, they default to what feels safest.

Safety for managers often looks like silence.

Silence for employees often looks like struggle.

Try a few shifts that don't require permission.

You don't need a policy update to improve how managers support people.

Managers can:

- Ask "what drains your energy here?" as well as "what motivates you?"
- Agree ways of working instead of assuming them
- Separate feedback on the work from feedback on style

- Revisit expectations regularly, not just at review time

None of this is special treatment.

It's basic management done deliberately.

Consistency doesn't mean sameness.

It means fairness over time.

A question to sit with before you move on

Before you turn the page, whether you manage people directly, or influence how management is set up, these are worth asking:

"If a manager avoided these conversations, who would end up carrying the cost instead"?

Because when managers don't feel supported to manage difference,

the burden doesn't disappear.

It just moves.

Conversation Starter:

"How do we make it safe for people to ask for what they need; without making them feel like an exception?"

. . .

One Small Experiment

Reframe This

Instead of: "They're asking for special treatment".

Try: "What barriers in our system are making it harder for this person to do their best work?"

How does this shift the conversation in your next performance or support discussion?

Chapter 8

Communication, conflict, and the hidden rules of work

Most workplace conflict isn't caused by disagreement.

It's caused by misunderstanding.

Not loud, dramatic misunderstanding either, but the quiet kind that builds over time. The kind where people stop giving each other the benefit of the doubt, where intent gets questioned, where tone becomes the focus instead of content, where someone slowly becomes labelled as "difficult", "abrupt", or "not quite right for the team".

Neurodivergent team members are disproportionately caught in this space; not because they communicate badly, but because they are often operating under a different set of assumptions, while everyone else believes the rules are obvious.

They aren't.

The rules nobody writes down

Every workplace has a parallel operating system.

It governs things like:

- How direct you're allowed to be
- Whether speed is valued over accuracy
- When silence means agreement and when it means disengagement
- Who can challenge whom, and how

These rules are rarely documented; they're learned through observation, correction, and sometimes, punishment.

For people who intuitively pick up social cues, this system feels invisible. For others, it feels arbitrary, inconsistent, and exhausting.

This is where many people start to self-edit: they soften emails, rewrite messages repeatedly, delay speaking until they're sure. Or go the other way, opting for precision and clarity, only to be told they're "too blunt".

The same behaviour can be praised or penalised depending on who delivers it.

I've written about this repeatedly, because once you experience it, it stays with you.

People aren't failing to communicate; they're being asked to operate inside a system that never explains its own rules.

In one organisation, directness is praised as efficiency. In another, the same behaviour is labelled abrasive. Silence might mean thoughtfulness in one team, disengagement in another. Asking questions might signal care, or incompetence.

They're rarely written down, but they still shape outcomes.

When rules aren't visible but still impact decision making, they inevitably favour the people who already fit.

When being clear and direct is misread as tone

This is the loop I see most often.

Someone says exactly what they mean.

Instead of focusing on the content, the listener focuses on how it sounded.

That reaction turns into an assumption:

"They're abrupt"

"They're annoyed"

"They're difficult"

Those assumptions get treated as intent.

Intent becomes a judgement about attitude or personality.

And that judgement doesn't stay in the moment.

It shows up later, in feedback, in trust, in who gets given the benefit of the doubt, and in who gets opportunities.

By the time feedback arrives, it's no longer about a piece of work; it's about who someone is perceived to be.

At that point, repairing the relationship is far harder than repairing the communication ever would have been.

Direct communication makes people uncomfortable; especially in cultures that value politeness over actually saying the thing.

When someone says exactly what they mean, without padding, softeners, or performance, it can be experienced as confrontational; not because it is, but because the listener is used to reading between the lines.

That's how intent gets distorted.

The message becomes secondary to its delivery.

The point is lost.

And over time, people stop collaborating and start managing each other instead.

That isn't working together.

It's emotional labour.

Conflict avoidance creates conflict

Many organisations pride themselves on being "nice".

They value harmony.

They avoid difficult conversations.

They encourage people to "take things offline" rather than deal with issues openly.

On the surface, that looks considerate.

In reality, it often stores problems rather than solving them.

Some of the most fragile teams I've worked with describe themselves as "nice".

What they often mean is conflict-avoidant.

Discomfort is pushed down the road or behind the curtains. Feedback is softened until it loses meaning. Tension is allowed to build because naming it feels impolite.

On the face of it, they appear to have a great culture.

But silence isn't a culture.

For people who rely on clarity to do good work, this environment is exhausting. You're constantly trying to work out what isn't being said, and whether you're already being judged for missing it.

Indirect feedback creates ambiguity.

Ambiguity creates anxiety.

Anxiety leads to over-correction or withdrawal.

And eventually, conflict.

What's framed as a communication problem is often a design problem.

The system doesn't tolerate difference in style, so individuals are expected to absorb the cost.

I know this because I've lived it.

When I was a young boy at school, I couldn't hold a pen properly.

Actually, I still can't.

I couldn't spell, and spelling is still a challenge today.

I also couldn't say my own name properly.

I'd say *Feo* instead of *Theo.*

I couldn't pronounce the "th".

Those things don't just disappear.

Neither does the trauma, the stigma, or the bullying that comes with them.

So even now, despite advising leadership teams, boards, governments, and universities, if I'm asked to pick up a pen and write on a board, my body reacts before my brain does.

I panic.

I'm suddenly back there.

Afraid I'll be found out.

That fight, flight, or freeze response is happening every day in organisations.

And we misread it in exactly the same way.

We label it as arrogance.

As disengagement.

As lack of ability.

When, in many cases, it's a stress response, not a capability issue.

So much of the conflict we see at work isn't interpersonal at all.

It's unresolved fear meeting systems that don't allow for difference.

As leaders, we need to step back; not to smooth things over, but to understand what's actually happening.

Because many people who appear to be "in conflict" aren't being difficult; they're in crisis.

What makes the difference isn't silence or confrontation; it's knowing when to step in, and how.

That's the moment people remember whether someone led with care, or just managed the issue.

Email, Slack, meetings: same problem, different formats

Digital communication was meant to make work easier. In some ways, it has. It gives people choice in how they communicate. It supports remote and flexible working. It allows clarity without interruption.

Choice of channel is often framed as flexibility, but without shared rules it becomes another system people have to decode.

And it's multiplied the system:

- Email
- Slack
- Teams
- WhatsApp
- Calendar invites

- Calls
- Texts

Each comes with its own unspoken expectations: where you should be, how quickly you should reply, what counts as urgent, what silence means.

Very few organisations ever make those rules explicit.

Written communication removes tone and context, yet expectations around speed and availability have only increased.

A delayed response is interpreted.

A short message is analysed.

Emojis become stand-ins for warmth or depending on culture and generation; evidence of being unprofessional or inappropriate.

For some people, clear written communication looks like what it is: concise, factual, to the point. In the wrong culture, that same clarity is reframed as disengagement, coldness, or lack of care.

Meetings create a different but related problem. Faster talkers dominate. Interruptions go unchecked. Thinking time is treated as hesitation. People who process internally are left trying to catch a moving conversation while also managing how they're being perceived.

The irony is that the same person who struggles to speak in the meeting may produce excellent written analysis afterwards. But by then, the decision has already been made.

So people lose out at both ends.

Too direct in writing, and they're misread.

Too slow to speak, and they're overlooked.

This isn't about preference or personality; it's about unclear rules.

When organisations offer multiple communication channels without shared expectations, they don't create flexibility; they create friction. People spend energy tracking platforms, second-guessing norms, and managing impressions instead of doing the work.

The problem isn't choice; it's choice without clear communication.

And once again, those who don't naturally infer the rules pay the highest price.

Labels are shortcuts, and they stick

Once communication differences are noticed, labels tend to follow.

"Difficult"

"Overly sensitive"

"Not very collaborative"

"Too intense"

These labels rarely come from a single incident.

They accumulate quietly, often without the person ever knowing they're being applied.

By the time feedback arrives, it's vague and historical.

Hard to respond to.

Harder still to undo.

What makes this especially damaging is that labels rarely trigger curiosity or support.

Nobody sits down and says, *"We're excluding this person."*

Instead, they stop being invited.

Stop being trusted with ambiguity.

Stop being considered for stretch work.

From the organisation's perspective, nothing dramatic happened.

From the individual's perspective, their world is closing in.

This is how capable people drift out of informal networks, high-visibility projects, and promotion conversations, without ever being told why.

And yet, labels aren't always the problem.

In the right context, they can be enabling.

An autism diagnosis can unlock support for a child in school: extra structure, adjustments in the classroom, understanding instead of punishment.

A dyslexic job applicant asking for extra time on a written assessment isn't asking for an advantage; they're asking for a fair chance in a process that relies heavily on reading and writing.

In those moments, the label creates access.

But in the workplace, labels often arrive without understanding.

A manager hears "autism" and what fills the gap is whatever they've absorbed from headlines or stereotypes; geniuses with photographic memories, savants, or people who need constant care.

None of which reflect the reality of most autistic adults at work.

So instead of opening doors, the label quietly reshapes expectations:

- What someone is trusted with
- How much margin for error they're given
- Whether their behaviour is interpreted generously or not

The label becomes a shortcut.

Not out of malice.

But out of lack of understanding.

And unchecked, those shortcuts can become toxic; not because people intend harm,

but because assumptions replace conversation.

This isn't about getting everything right.

It's about noticing when a label has taken over, and being willing to pause long enough to ask what support actually helps.

Making communication safer without sanitising it

Improving communication doesn't mean forcing everyone to communicate the same way.

It means:

- Making expectations explicit
- Normalising different styles

- Separating *what* is said from *how* it's said
- Addressing issues early, before they calcify into stories

Teams that do this well don't rely on mind-reading; they agree how they'll work together.

That might include:

- Clear norms around response times
- Permission to ask for clarification without judgement
- Explicit meeting structures that allow different forms of contribution
- Feedback that focuses on outcomes, not personality

None of this requires training budgets or culture programmes; it requires intention.

A simple working agreement goes a long way

Not a values poster.

Not a mission statement.

And not something written once, laminated, and forgotten.

A working agreement is a practical, lived reference point.

It surfaces things people are usually too unsure to ask out loud.

Questions like:

- How do we give feedback here?
- Directly or indirectly? In the moment or later?
- What happens when something isn't clear?
- Do we ask immediately, or are we expected to "figure it out"?
- How do we handle disagreement?
- Is challenge welcomed, tolerated, or quietly penalised?
- What does respect actually look like in practice?
- In meetings. In messages. Under pressure.

When these things are named, tension drops.

People stop wasting energy trying to read between the lines.

Miscommunication becomes easier to repair because it's no longer personal; it's contextual.

For neurodivergent team members, this can be transformative.

Instead of having to decode tone, hierarchy, or unspoken expectations, the rules of engagement are visible.

But this isn't just about neurodivergence.

Everyone benefits when the guessing stops.

What's often missed is that this doesn't have to be an organisation-wide rulebook to work.

In fact, some of the most effective examples I've seen live at team level.

In many organisations, teams already operate in their own microclimates. You can feel it physically. I've worked in places where walking into the tech team felt like stepping out of open fields and into the trees. Suddenly the environment changes: daily stand-ups, emotional support and wellbeing objects on desks, mood boards, strategy trees on the walls, adaptive lighting, noise dampening.

Sometimes they're even on a completely different floor.

Those teams didn't always get there through policy. They experimented. They adjusted. They named what worked for them. And over time, some of those ways of working spilled out into the rest of the organisation. Other teams borrowed ideas, adapted them, made them their own.

That's important, because it shows this isn't about enforcing sameness; it's about making differences explicit.

A working agreement doesn't say "this is how everyone must work".

It says "this is how *we* work, for now".

And it leaves room for that to evolve.

What matters here isn't the document itself; it's the signal it sends.

A working agreement says:

"We don't expect you to mind-read"

"We'll name how we work"

"And if something isn't working, we can revisit it"

That shift is subtle, but powerful.

When teams are willing to name how they operate, rather than expecting people to infer it, communication stops being a test of belonging and starts being a way of getting work done.

And when that happens, energy goes back into the work itself, instead of into managing uncertainty.

"How best to work with me" - making the invisible visible

One simple extension of a team working agreement is a short "how best to work with me" note.

Not a diagnosis.

Not a list of needs.

And not something written for HR.

It's a practical, optional snapshot that answers a very human question:

If you want me at my best, here's what helps.

For some people, this might be a few bullet points.

For others, a short paragraph.

The format matters far less than the intent.

A good "working with me" note might cover things like:

- How I prefer to receive feedback
- What helps me think clearly under pressure
- How I like to communicate when something's unclear
- What drains my energy faster than people realise
- What support looks like when I'm stretched, not failing.

This isn't about lowering expectations.

It's about reducing the everyday friction we all feel.

When managers and teammates understand these things early, fewer assumptions are made later.

People don't have to guess whether silence means thinking or disengagement.

Directness isn't misread as attitude.

Support isn't delayed until someone is already in distress.

For those who've already faced numerous barriers across their life and career, either physical, emotional, or neurological; this can be especially powerful.

It creates a way to explain differences in working style without having to repeatedly justify them.

It shifts the conversation from *what's wrong* to *what works*.

But again, this isn't special treatment.

Everyone has conditions under which they do their best work.

Most teams just never talk about them.

What matters is choice.

A "how best to work with me" note should never be forced.

And it should never become static.

Like disclosure, it's a living thing.

What helps now might not help in six months.

Roles change. Energy changes. Context changes.

The value isn't in getting it perfect.

It's in making it normal to talk about how work actually happens, before misunderstandings harden into problems.

When teams make space for this level of clarity, working relationships become less fragile.

People spend less time managing impressions, and more time contributing.

And work starts to feel less like a performance, and more like a collaboration.

Conflict isn't the enemy, silence is

I once worked in an organisation where everyone was *lovely* to each other; kind, polite, endlessly agreeable, while completely avoiding the fact that we were on a sinking ship.

It honestly felt like being the brass band on the Titanic; everyone playing their part, smiling, keeping the mood light, as the ship slowly disappeared beneath us.

Most of the conflict organisations fear is already happening.

It's just happening internally, in people's heads, rather than out loud where it can be named, tested, and resolved.

Neuroinclusive teams don't avoid that tension; they name it early, notice when something hasn't landed, and reset before it becomes personal.

As a result, tension is expected and worked through; not avoided or quietly turned into judgement.

In these teams, people are allowed to say:

"That didn't land the way I intended"

"I need more clarity here"

"I think we're talking past each other"

Those moments aren't treated as failure; they're treated as part of working things out together.

Crucially, repair happens early, before misunderstandings turn into stories about attitude or intent.

It hopefully means the ship doesn't sink!

This doesn't mean anything goes.

It doesn't mean lowering standards or tiptoeing around performance.

It means standards are clear.

And communication isn't used to police behaviour.

The work is what matters.

And when something does go wrong, the focus is on fixing the issue, not labelling the person.

Because the people who challenge the status quo and push boundaries are also the ones most likely to fail; often and early.

When we label *them* as the problem, we don't reduce risk. We remove the appetite for it. And what we're left with isn't safety; it's conformity, for conformity's sake.

Silence, by contrast, looks calm but carries a cost.

Unspoken frustration doesn't disappear.

It just leaks out sideways, through tone, distance, and quiet exclusion.

Teams that can repair don't avoid discomfort; they shorten the time people spend stuck in it.

And that ability, to notice, name, and reset; is one of the most practical forms of care a manager can offer.

Designing for difference means naming the rules

Most communication breakdowns don't need mediation. They just need naming.

Problems escalate not because people disagree, but because they're operating with different assumptions and no shared reference point.

One person thinks speed signals commitment. Another thinks accuracy matters more. One assumes silence means agreement. Another assumes it means space to think.

None of that is malicious; it's just unspoken.

When the rules of communication stay implicit, only the people who already understand them get to relax. Everyone else has to guess. Guessing takes energy. And energy spent guessing is energy not spent contributing.

This is often where people get labelled:

"Too blunt"

"Too vague"

"Too sensitive"

"Hard to read"

Those labels rarely describe ability; they describe friction between a person and an unarticulated system.

People who process differently tend to carry the cost of that friction first, because the margin for misinterpretation is smaller. But they are never the only ones affected. Over time, these unspoken rules limit everyone. They narrow who speaks up, who challenges, and who feels safe being precise instead of performative.

When teams name how they communicate, something shifts.

Expectations become clearer.

Missteps become easier to repair.

Conflict becomes less personal, because it's no longer about intent; it's about alignment.

Work stops being a test of social fluency and starts becoming what it should have been all along: a place where contribution matters more than performance, and clarity replaces guesswork.

Designed for Human Action

(How to reduce friction without flattening difference)

Most workplace communication problems don't announce themselves as problems.

They show up as tone debates.

As awkward follow-ups.

As stories people tell about each other when the work itself hasn't changed.

By the time something is labelled "conflict", it's usually been brewing for a while.

So rather than asking, *"How do we communicate better?"*

Start by asking, *"Where are we asking people to guess?"*

That's where things usually go wrong.

Start with the moments people keep explaining away

Listen for the phrases that signal misalignment rather than malice:

"They didn't mean it like that"

"They're very direct"

"They just don't read the room"

"That's not how we usually do things"

When the same explanations keep appearing; it's not a personality issue.

It's a sign that expectations are living in people's heads instead of the system.

Unspoken rules don't create harmony; they create insiders and outsiders.

Shift the focus from tone to intent

A lot of unnecessary friction comes from treating tone as evidence:

Short messages become "cold".

Silence becomes "disengagement".

Precision becomes "abrasiveness".

Instead of reacting to *how* something landed, get curious about *what* was meant:

"What was the point you were trying to make?"

"What would have helped that land more clearly?"

"Where did the signal get lost here?"

That small shift, from judgement to clarification, prevents most conflicts from escalating.

Make a few things explicit that are usually left vague

You don't need a team charter or a communications workshop to do this.

Just name the things people currently have to infer:

- How quickly people are expected to respond
- What "urgent" actually means in practice
- When disagreement is welcome, and how it should show up

- What silence usually signals here: thinking, agreement, or overload

When people don't know the rules of engagement, they default to self-protection.

Self-protection looks like withdrawal, or defensiveness, or friction.

Normalise repair, not perfection

Neuroinclusive teams aren't conflict-free; they're able to repair on the move.

They make space for:

- "That didn't land how I meant it to"
- "I need more clarity before responding"
- "Can we reset this conversation"

When repair is normalised, people don't have to mask or over-manage every interaction; they can focus on the work instead of the performance.

One question worth carrying forward

Before you move on, sit with this:

"When communication breaks down here, do we treat it as a failure of character, or a signal that the system stayed silent?"

Because communication rarely fails in dramatic moments.

It fails quietly, in the gaps between what's said, what's meant, and what's assumed.

And those gaps are designable.

Conversation Starter:

"What's one unspoken rule about communication here that you wish was made explicit?"

Chapter 9

Career progression: why capability stalls without fitting in

Most organisations think neurodiversity is a hiring problem.

It isn't.

People were always there. They were hired, promoted into roles, trusted with responsibility. What they weren't given was sustained support, clarity, or room to grow without burning out.

In fact, for many autistic people, access to work has become harder, not easier. During and since Covid, large numbers lost roles, struggled to return, or found themselves quietly excluded by new expectations around speed, visibility, and constant availability.

The problem isn't that neurodivergent talent suddenly appeared, and organisations didn't know what to do with them. The problem is that systems were never built to support them once the pressure increased.

So this isn't just a hiring issue.

It's a progression and sustainability issue.

I've spoken to countless people who didn't leave because something went wrong.

They left because nothing changed.

They were hired, relied on, and then left to plateau. Development stalled. Feedback became vague. Opportunity doors closed. They became the person who held things together, who fixed problems, who absorbed complexity, but whose name never came up when growth, promotion, or stretch roles were discussed.

To everyone else, it felt abrupt.

To them, it had been building quietly for a long time.

They hadn't checked out because they didn't care.

They checked out because the path ahead had disappeared.

The myth of the stalled individual

When someone stops progressing, we tend to look inward:

"They're not quite ready"

"They lack confidence"

"They don't put themselves forward enough"

"They're great where they are"

These explanations feel reasonable because they locate the issue in the individual.

They're also convenient, because they let systems off the hook.

I write about this often, across my newsletters and talks, because I see the same pattern repeat.

High-performing neurodivergent people are rarely failing.

They are delivering; often consistently, sometimes exceptionally.

What they are *not* doing is performing potential in the way organisations expect.

And that distinction matters.

Potential isn't just about what someone might do next.

It's about whether decision-makers can *see* that future in them; whether they can imagine that person in the room, in the role, at the table.

When decisions are based on who people can picture,

rather than what people have done, progression stops being fair; and it certainly stops being transparent.

People promote what feels familiar.

They trust what looks like themselves.

And when that happens, capability can be overlooked not because it isn't there, but because it doesn't present itself in the expected image.

This becomes most visible when the context changes:

A new manager arrives.

A restructure happens.

A team is reformed.

Processes shift.

The value that was once *felt,* through everyday moments, small decisions, quiet problem-solving, and unspoken contribution; was never written down, never made visible, never protected by the system.

It wasn't etched into performance frameworks or carved into HR stone.

It lived in relationships, trust, and accumulated understanding.

When that context goes, the organisation often realises

how little of that contribution was ever formally recognised.

Almost overnight, someone who was delivering becomes "unproven".

Someone who was trusted becomes "a risk"; not because their ability changed, but because the system no longer knows how to see it.

That's when people become vulnerable; not because they stopped working, but because their progression was never designed to survive change.

How "potential" quietly filters people out

Potential is one of the most powerful, and least examined, ideas in working life.

It sounds positive.

Encouraging.

Fair.

But most of us have seen what happens when potential doesn't turn into the shape others expected.

Think about the young sports star everyone was sure would "make it"; the one talked about as a future international, until an injury, a bad season, or simply a change in circumstances knocked them off course.

Or the artist on your degree course, the one tutors quietly revered as *the* future, who now works in corporate sales.

Or the person you sat next to in maths class, the one everyone assumed would go on to crack codes or build something world-changing, who now scans barcodes in a supermarket.

There's no judgement here. All work has value. And hopefully those people are happy, fulfilled, and living lives that make sense to them.

I've felt the weight of potential personally.

In the late 90s, I spent around eight years as a member of the Sherman Youth Theatre in Cardiff. It was led by an inspiring, disruptive youth theatre director, Andrew Loretto, who genuinely believed in young people and pushed us hard. We had one standout year in particular; creatively, culturally, publicly.

That year culminated in performances on some of the biggest stages we'd ever touched. Local and national newspapers picked up our performances over the years. One review even said: *"If these are the future stars of the West End, book me a seat in 2010."*

You can still find me on the Sherman Theatres website as part of their history timeline, there I am, along with several others to highlight the success of the school of

1999. Although you might not recognise me in my strange costume of yellow swimming goggles, a decorator's jump suit, and a feather duster for headwear!

That's potential. Nationally validated. Publicly celebrated.

But it didn't come with a golden ticket.

It didn't unlock the invisible networks, the financial safety nets, the informal sponsorship, or the unspoken knowledge about how to turn promise into a sustainable career. For a very small number of people, they may hold the secret key; often power and privilege. For most of us, that moment of potential slowly dissipated; not because the talent vanished, but because the pathways did.

And that's the part we rarely talk about. Potential without access doesn't compound; it fades.

Looking back, that experience taught me something I see in life and in workplaces. Potential isn't just about ability; it's about proximity to opportunity, fluency in unwritten rules, and being handed the keys at the right moment. Very few people are. Most are expected to work it out alone.

Which is why "potential" carries such weight, and such risk. When we celebrate it without building the structures that allow it to grow, we don't just set unrealistic expectations; we quietly filter people out, while telling ourselves we gave them a chance.

But "potential" has a lot to answer for.

Because it carries weight.

And that weight is rarely shared evenly.

In workplaces, potential often becomes a shorthand for things that are easier to spot than to justify. It quietly rewards:

- Confidence over competence
- Visibility over value
- Fluency over depth
- Comfort with ambiguity over clarity

Potential is usually discussed behind closed doors; in succession meetings, in quiet conversations about who feels "ready" or who has "more runway". It's assessed without clear evidence, rarely challenged, and heavily shaped by familiarity.

This isn't malicious.

It's human.

But when progression depends on subjective signals rather than observable contribution, sameness wins. People who don't perform potential in the expected way, who are steady rather than shiny, precise rather than expansive, thoughtful rather than loud; slowly fall out of view.

What makes this particularly painful is that many of those people are still delivering; still holding things together, still relied on when the work gets complex or fragile. They haven't failed. They've just stopped being seen as next.

Over time, that gap becomes impossible to ignore.

Left unchecked, potential turns into a shortcut; it lifts a few people by name, while others fade quietly into the background.

And the people it elevates aren't always supported; they're simply watched more closely, expected more of, and left to cope.

It doesn't build futures.

It burns people out.

Nobody comes out ahead.

Visibility is not value, but it's treated like it is

Many neurodivergent people contribute a huge amount to teams and organisations, but they do it quietly, without fanfare or the need to be noticed.

They solve complex problems.

They stabilise systems.

They improve quality.

They prevent errors nobody ever sees.

But this kind of contribution doesn't always translate into visibility; especially in cultures that reward self-promotion, spontaneity, and presence in the room.

I've written and spoken about this before; how being *seen* often matters more than being *useful*.

Not because outcomes don't matter, but because confidence often speaks louder than results.

This creates a perverse incentive.

People who talk well about work progress faster than people who quietly do the work well.

It took me over 35 years to realise how deeply I'd internalised this.

For most of my life, I gave 110% of my energy; not just to work, but to people, conversations, projects, events, anywhere that would take it.

Work hard.

Play hard.

Die hard.

Not the Hollywood version.

The flat-on-the-sofa, can't-move, wondering-what-just-happened version.

What I didn't understand for a long time was the connection between how I lived and how I felt. I burned through time, money, energy, ideas; as if they'd expire if I didn't use them all up.

Here's the irony:

AI can save me time.

But time was never the real problem.

I'll always fill time; I'm very good at that.

Time is just a bucket with a hole in it.

Energy, though?

Where I put that matters.

Being first in and last out can feel good.

It fills a gap.

It gives purpose.

But being first in and last out of *everything;* work, ideas, events, relationships, comes with a cost.

And this is where visibility culture becomes dangerous.

When constant availability is mistaken for commitment,

when presence is mistaken for value,

people learn to perform contribution rather than protect their capacity.

For people operating with less margin for error, this can become a trap.

You over-give to stay visible.

You stay visible to stay safe.

And slowly, sustainability erodes.

So the question isn't whether people are contributing enough; it's whether the system knows how to *see* contribution without exhausting the people delivering it.

If AI can help us optimise time,

we still need leaders and managers who understand energy.

Because visibility isn't value.

And work that only rewards what can be seen will always miss what actually holds everything together.

Mentoring isn't enough

Mentoring and coaching both have an important role to

play, especially for people who've spent years adapting themselves to systems that didn't adapt in return.

Mentors help people understand the landscape.

Coaches help people understand themselves.

That support matters.

But it doesn't change what happens when decisions are made without the person in the room.

That's why support alone isn't enough.

Progression requires advocacy.

Mentors help people think things through.

They offer advice.

They help you prepare, rehearse, and reflect.

All of that has value.

But it doesn't shape what happens when your name comes up behind closed doors.

That's where sponsorship shows itself.

Because when no one speaks on your behalf, something else always fills the gap:

Assumptions, half-remembered impressions, or silence.

And as we've discussed in previous chapters, silence rarely helps anyone.

When organisations notice progression gaps, mentoring is often the first solution offered.

It feels safe. Supportive. Well-intentioned.

And for many people, it genuinely helps.

But mentoring doesn't move power.

Sponsorship does.

Sponsors don't just coach from the sidelines.

They advocate when the person isn't there.

They put someone forward for opportunities that haven't been advertised yet.

They translate contribution into language that decision-makers recognise and trust.

They say things like:

"I've seen them handle complexity"

"They're ready for more than they're being given"

"I'd back them in this role"

That kind of advocacy changes outcomes.

Those who've been on the margins; whether through neurodivergence, race, gender, age, or class, are less likely to be sponsored. Not due to a lack of ability, but because sponsorship is built on ease and familiarity;

and familiarity usually mirrors what's already in the room.

People sponsor those who feel predictable to them; those whose style they recognise, those they wouldn't have to explain.

And it isn't just employees.

People in leadership positions who think differently are often less visible too.

They may not self-promote in the expected ways.

They may do their best work behind the scenes, or avoid the informal spaces where sponsorship relationships usually form.

So even when someone is actively looking for a sponsor, or when a manager is trying to help them find one, the options can feel limited.

Not because capability is missing, but because visibility has been narrowly defined.

The more we normalise difference, and the more openly we value neurodiversity at every level, the easier it becomes for people to recognise each other.

And when recognition improves, sponsorship stops being accidental.

It becomes possible.

Which is why capable people so often end up well-mentored but quietly unsponsored.

Prepared, but not progressed.

Ready, but unseen at the point where decisions are actually made.

That's why mentoring alone doesn't close progression gaps.

It helps individuals cope with the system.

Sponsorship changes how the system responds to them.

And if organisations are serious about unlocking future potential, especially potential that doesn't announce itself; they need to pay attention to who is being spoken *for*, not just who is being spoken *to*.

The cost of being forced to stay where you are

Staying where you are shouldn't be a problem.

For many people, it's the right choice.

They have caring responsibilities; young children, elderly parents, health needs, lives that demand stability rather than stretch.

Doing a job well, consistently, over time should carry value.

It should be respected.

Rewarded.

And seen as a contribution in its own right.

Not every path forward needs to point towards promotion.

Not every form of progression needs to end in management.

We've all seen what happens when it does: the brilliant painter and decorator who's pushed into managing other painters, the practitioner who loves doing the work, forced into designing or overseeing it instead.

Sometimes progression doesn't elevate people; it pulls them away from what they're good at, and what they love to do.

And yes, work is changing. Skills evolve. Technology shifts.

We all need to keep learning to stay relevant.

But *how fast* we change, *how far* we stretch, and *in which direction* shouldn't be decided for people.

Progression isn't one ladder.

And it shouldn't only move from A to Z.

Where this becomes damaging is when staying put stops being a choice.

Being told you're "valuable where you are" can sound like praise.

In the moment, it often is.

But when you *want* to grow, adapt, or try something new, and find that encouragement quietly disappears; that reassurance starts to land differently.

Over time, it becomes a ceiling.

What's framed as appreciation slowly sends another message:

You're useful here.

Just not elsewhere.

For people who've already faced barriers, because of disability, age, race, gender, background, or difference, the response is often not disengagement, but adjustment.

They narrow their ambition.

They stop pushing.

They stop applying.

They stop putting themselves forward for stretch or progression.

Instead, they focus on delivery.

They tell themselves stability is enough.

That progression isn't that important anyway.

This isn't a lack of drive.

It's self-protection.

When effort isn't recognised, conserving energy becomes necessary.

When ambition carries risk but little reward, pulling back is rational.

This is how organisations lose future capability without ever noticing.

No resignation letter.

No performance issue.

No dramatic exit.

Just a quiet recalibration.

Ambition doesn't disappear.

It adapts.

People stop raising their hand.

Stop imagining a future there.

Stop seeing themselves as "next", even when they're more than capable.

From the organisation's perspective, it can look like loyalty.

Or contentment.

Or making space for others.

From the employee's perspective, it feels like their career has slowly hit the brakes.

And once someone starts designing their life around staying where they are,

it becomes much harder to imagine moving again; even when the opportunity finally arrives.

A familiar organisational story

I've seen this play out more times than I can count.

A neurodivergent employee is well regarded; reliable, knowledgeable, often the person others turn to when things go wrong...

They carry institutional memory; the one that knows the quirky systems nobody else understands.

They stabilise teams, by bringing a natural balance, filling gaps others don't even see.

They make other people's work easier, usually without drawing attention to it.

But when promotion conversations happen, the language shifts.

They're described as:

- Not quite ready, need more time.
- Lacking gravitas, that special something, you just know it when you see it.
- Needing to be more strategic, a leader, speaks up more, you know the drill!

None of this is written down.

None of it is measurable.

And none of it is discussed directly with the person concerned.

There's no clear feedback to respond to.

No development plan to engage with, or work towards.

Just a sense that the bar keeps moving, quietly and out of reach.

The system never says no.

It just never quite says yes either.

That's what makes these progression systems so hard to challenge.

There's no process to challenge.

No moment to interrogate.

No single conversation where the criteria are laid bare.

Just a gradual loss of momentum that's difficult to name, and even harder to prove.

And the sad reality! When a crisis hits, it's often these same people who stay; who lean in, who carry the weight, even as their own future quietly gets ignored.

Progression systems reflect values, not intentions

Career pathways are one of the clearest signals of what an organisation truly values.

If progression requires:

- Political navigation
- Informal networks
- Ambiguous signals
- Self-advocacy without support

Then progression will always skew towards those most comfortable operating that way.

Neuroinclusive organisations don't abandon standards; they make them visible.

They define what progression looks like in practice.

They separate leadership capability from performance theatre.

They ensure contribution is translated, not assumed.

Designing progression that doesn't rely on sameness

Better progression systems:

- Make criteria explicit
- Value outcomes over style
- Actively counter familiarity bias
- Hold leaders accountable for who they sponsor

This isn't about guaranteeing advancement; it's about guaranteeing fairness of opportunity.

When people understand how progression works, they can decide how to engage with it. When they don't, only those who already fit thrive.

Drift is a choice

No organisation sets out to stall capable people.

Very few leaders wake up intending to block progress.

But when progression systems are left to drift, they don't remain fair.

They default to what feels safe, familiar, recognisable.

Good intentions don't prevent predictable outcomes.

When criteria are vague, familiarity fills the gap.

When evidence is messy, comfort slides into decision making.

And when no one is explicitly accountable for progression, inertia quietly takes over.

Career stagnation isn't hard to explain.

It's what happens when systems quietly reward people who fit the mould, while pretending everyone's being treated the same.

That's why the same types of people keep moving.

And why others are repeatedly told to wait; not overtly, but implicitly.

Design can change that.

But only if organisations are willing to look honestly at their own patterns:

Who keeps being stretched.

Who keeps being sponsored.

And who keeps being reassured instead.

There's no single decision to appeal.

No clear moment to interrogate.

No email, meeting, or policy you can point to and say, *"that's where it happened"*.

Momentum drains away quietly, without any clear moment to challenge.

And by the time it becomes visible,

the drift has already done its work.

Designed for Human Action

(How to recognise contribution before it disappears)

Most organisations say they want more diverse talent at senior levels.

Fewer are willing to look closely at how people actually progress once they're inside.

Careers rarely stall because someone stops contributing.

They stall because contribution stops being recognised in ways the system understands.

If this chapter has made you slightly uncomfortable, that's probably the point.

Here's where to start.

First, notice what you've learned to explain away.

Listen to the language that shows up when progression stalls:

"They're brilliant, but they don't put themselves forward"

"They need to be more visible"

"They're great where they are"

When the same people consistently deliver but never quite move, confidence isn't the problem; measurement is.

If progression depends on self-promotion, informal advocacy, or fitting an unspoken leadership mould, difference will always lose; quietly and repeatedly.

Next, stop trying to fix people and look at the system instead.

Don't coach someone to *perform* leadership in a way that only works for a narrow group.

Redesign how progression decisions are made.

Ask yourself, honestly:

- Where do we rely on reputation rather than evidence
- Whose names get spoken for when they're not in the room, and whose don't
- Which behaviours are genuinely rewarded, and which are just tolerated until they become inconvenient

Career progression isn't a reward for endurance; it's a system. And like any system, it produces predictable outcomes.

When pathways are unclear, people either burn energy trying to decode them or quietly disengage.

Neither of those outcomes is a talent problem.

If you try one thing differently, try this.

In your next progression or promotion conversation, pause and ask:

"What evidence are we actually using here, and what assumptions are filling the gaps?"

Because the moment you make progression criteria explicit, you don't lower the bar.

You make it visible.

And when people can see how the system works, they can decide how, or whether, to engage with it.

That's not special treatment.

That's fair and transparent design.

Conversation Starter:

"Who in our organisation quietly delivers, but rarely gets noticed or sponsored for new opportunities?"

Chapter 10

Designed for humans (or not at all)

By this point in the book, one thing should be clear.

Most workplace problems aren't caused by difficult people.

They're caused by decisions that once felt sensible, reasonable, even well-intentioned.

Processes were put in place to create fairness.

Shortcuts were taken to save time.

Rules were introduced to reduce risk.

Over time, those choices turned into "just how things are done".

And when the world changed, how people work, communicate, process information, recover; the systems didn't always change with it.

That's why the same issues keep reappearing, with different people, in different roles, across different organisations.

This matters, because it changes where responsibility sits.

Not with individuals who struggle inside these systems,

but with the choices that shaped them, and the willingness to revisit those choices now.

Systems don't fail by accident

Earlier in the book, I talked about the Mexican tetra fish.

Not as a curiosity, but as a reminder: when environments change, what looks like deficiency in one context becomes adaptation in another.

The fish didn't fail.

The environment changed what mattered.

Work is no different.

Most exclusion at work isn't malicious.

But it *is* created and shaped but those in roles of responsibility.

Recruitment filters people out because someone decided what "good" looked like.

Onboarding overwhelms people because speed was prioritised over clarity.

Managers hesitate because nobody showed them how to support difference without risk.

None of this happened by accident.

It happened through choices that were never revisited.

Inclusion isn't missing, it's mislocated

Most organisations believe inclusion lives in:

Policies.

Statements.

Training programmes.

ERGs.

Those things matter. But they aren't where inclusion is *felt*.

Inclusion lives in:

- How work is structured
- How decisions are made
- How ambiguity is handled
- What happens when someone doesn't fit the default, the line in the text book.

This is why so many organisations mean well and still see the same outcomes.

They invest in intention, but not in infrastructure.

When good intentions stall progress

One of the most consistent themes across my work is this:

"We didn't know" is no longer a valid position.

The evidence exists.

The stories are everywhere.

The patterns repeat across sectors.

What stalls progress isn't awareness; it's follow-through.

Inclusion efforts slow down when:

- Responsibility is diffused
- Ownership is unclear
- Change is optional

People don't experience those gaps as abstract ideas and thoughts; they experience them as daily friction, that over time can become disabling.

Most leaders don't ignore impact because they don't

care; they miss it because they've become conditioned to how things work.

I was reminded of this on a speed awareness course.

The police didn't lecture us about rules; they showed us what happens when a car hits a child at 20 miles an hour, then at 30, then at 40.

As a parent, that changed everything.

Nothing about my values shifted.

My perception did.

They also showed how little time is saved driving at 80mph or even 90 instead of 70 over a long journey. Once you see the numbers, the story you tell yourself about "efficiency" starts to fall apart.

That's what insight does; it dismantles assumptions we didn't even realise we were carrying.

Leaders don't need more pressure to care; they need clearer sight of the consequences their everyday choices create.

Because meaningful change rarely starts with tools or technology.

It starts when people see differently.

And once they do, they choose differently.

Systems shape behaviour

People don't behave randomly at work.

They adapt to what the environment quietly asks of them.

Not what's written in policies.

Not what's said in values statements.

But what actually gets rewarded, avoided, or ignored day to day.

If success requires:

- Masking
- Over-communication
- Constant self-regulation
- Guessing unspoken rules

Then people will do those things; not because they're incapable, but because they're trying to survive and succeed in the conditions they're given.

Those who don't adapt in these ways are often read differently.

They're described as challenging, difficult, not quite the right fit.

Not because they lack capability, but because they aren't

performing the behaviours the environment quietly expects.

This adaptation is rarely conscious.

It happens slowly, through pattern and consequence.

You notice who gets interrupted and who doesn't, who gets praised for being "visible", whose mistakes are forgiven and whose are remembered, which questions are welcomed and which create discomfort.

Over time, people adjust.

They learn when to speak, when to hold back, how much of themselves is safe to show.

They become fluent in the environment, even when that fluency comes at a cost.

This is why so many so-called performance issues seem to appear in the same teams, the same roles, the same functions.

It's not that capability disappears at random.

It's that certain environments consistently demand more compensation than others.

When capable people struggle in predictable ways, fatigue, withdrawal, over-preparation, missed promotion, quiet disengagement, it isn't coincidence.

And it isn't weakness; it's a sign that the conditions themselves are doing some of the work.

People aren't failing to meet the system; they're being shaped by its design.

And unless those conditions are examined, organisations will keep diagnosing individuals for problems that were created much earlier; long before anyone's performance was questioned.

Leadership without shame

This is where tone matters.

Because most leaders don't need to be told they're doing harm; they already carry a quiet awareness that things aren't quite working as intended.

They feel it in the difficult conversations they postpone, in the feedback they soften until it loses meaning, in the adjustments they know would help, but worry might open a door they don't know how to close.

Blame doesn't help here; it pushes people into defence.

Shame doesn't either; it creates silence, not change.

What does help is responsibility, not as a moral judgement, but as a practical one.

Designing work for humans doesn't require perfection; it requires honesty.

Honesty about where systems no longer match reality, about which behaviours are being rewarded by default, and about who is quietly carrying the cost when things don't quite fit.

That kind of honesty isn't comfortable.

But it's what makes progress possible.

It allows leaders to say, *"This made sense once. It doesn't anymore",* and to adjust without needing to justify the past or defend intent.

This isn't about shame.

It's about looking after the people and work in your care.

Because leadership isn't proved by getting everything right first time; it shows up in the willingness to notice, to revisit, and to change course when the consequences become clear.

Small changes compound

The things that actually improve work rarely feel dramatic.

You just realise one day that it's a bit easier than it was.

Someone explains expectations properly instead of assuming people will just "pick it up".

A process becomes predictable; not because it's perfect, but because it stops changing every five minutes.

Flexibility stops being something you have to earn, or justify, or apologise for.

None of that lowers the bar.

It just stops people wasting energy on things that shouldn't be hard in the first place.

When work is clearer, people spend less time second-guessing.

When processes are steady, they stop bracing themselves for surprises.

When flexibility is built in, people don't have to perform resilience just to get through the week.

On their own, these changes can look small; almost too small to bother with.

But they add up.

Less tension in meetings.

Fewer misunderstandings.

People having a bit more left at the end of the day to

think, to care, to do the job properly rather than just survive it.

People who experience work differently often feel this shift first. The relief is immediate.

But it doesn't stop with them.

Teams settle.

Decisions get better.

Performance becomes something you can sustain, not sprint towards until something breaks.

That's how most progress happens; not through a big transformation programme or a shiny new tool, but through a series of small, deliberate choices that slowly change what work feels like.

And once work starts feeling different, behaviour follows.

The choice organisations keep making

Every organisation is already making a choice:

Not always consciously.

Not always deliberately.

But every day, through what gets fixed and what gets tolerated.

You see it daily:

A new starter struggles, so a colleague quietly stays late to help them catch up.

A manager notices confusion but decides it's quicker to "just explain it again" than fix the process; someone builds a spreadsheet, a workaround, a personal system to cope with something that was never quite thought through.

None of this looks like big decisions.

But over time, a pattern appears and expectation sets in.

Either they keep compensating for systems that don't quite work, or systems start carrying more of the load.

Most organisations default to the first option; not because it's better, but because it's easier.

People step in.

They smooth things over.

They absorb the friction so the work keeps moving.

High performers become shock absorbers.

Conscientious people become the glue.

Those who care most quietly take on the extra work of making things function.

At an organisational level, everything looks fine.

Deadlines are met.

Clients are happy.

The organisation tells itself the system works.

What's harder to see is the cost:

The same people always staying late.

The same names popping up in "can you just…" messages.

The same individuals burning energy compensating for gaps that never get addressed.

Eventually, something gives.

People disengage.

They narrow their ambition.

They leave.

And when they do, organisations are often surprised, because the system *appeared* to be working right up until it didn't.

Choosing not to revisit how work is set up is still a decision; it just hides behind habit.

The alternative isn't radical.

It doesn't require tearing everything down.

It's the slower, less glamorous work of asking:

- Why does this rely on personal effort every time
- Why does this only function because someone goes above and beyond
- What would it look like if the system carried more of this load instead

That's the real choice.

Not between caring and not caring, but between repeatedly asking people to compensate, or finally letting the work support the people doing it.

And organisations make that choice whether they name it or not.

What "good" looks like

By this point, it should be clear that "good" doesn't mean perfect.

Good organisations still get things wrong.

They still have pressure, disagreement, missed signals, moments of friction.

The difference is what happens next.

In healthier environments, problems don't immediately get personalised.

The first question isn't *"Who's struggling?"*, it's *"What's making this harder than it needs to be?"*

Assumptions get revisited, not defended.

Processes get questioned when they stop working, rather than quietly endured.

Friction isn't ignored or normalised; it's treated as information.

Managers aren't left to improvise inclusion on top of everything else.

They're equipped with clarity, support, and permission to name when something isn't working, without it being framed as failure.

And when someone is struggling, the organisation looks outward before it looks inward.

Not every time.

Not perfectly.

But often enough that people feel the difference.

Good organisations understand something subtle but important:

inclusion isn't a programme you complete, or a value you announce.

It's revealed in the work, the daily tasks, how people communicate.

In how often people are left guessing what's expected of them.

In whether flexibility is assumed or negotiated.

In whether people are trusted before they've proved they can suffer in silence.

You can usually feel it.

Work feels steadier.

Less performative.

People spend more time doing the job, and less time managing how they're seen while doing it.

That doesn't make the work easier.

It makes it more visible.

And over time, those small, unglamorous choices add up.

Fewer people burn out quietly.

Fewer problems get mislabelled as attitude or capability.

More energy goes into progress, rather than self-protection.

That's what "good" looks like in practice.

Not an absence of challenge, but an environment where challenge doesn't require people to carry unnecessary cost just to stay in the room.

A final thought to leave with you

Neurodiversity doesn't make work harder.

Poorly designed work does.

Once you see that, it's difficult to ignore.

The question isn't whether work *should* be more inclusive; it's whether organisations are willing to take responsibility for the environments they've created, and reshape them for the humans who use them every day.

That's what this chapter has been about.

Not fixing people.

Fixing work.

Designed for Human Action

(How to stay human while systems scale)

Designing work that fits humans isn't a one-off initiative; it's an ongoing responsibility.

Most organisations don't fail because they don't care; they fail because they keep reusing systems that no longer match the reality of how people think, work, and live.

This is where leadership shows up; not in statements, but in design.

. . .

Where inclusion gets parked instead of practised

Inclusion often gets treated as a separate conversation:

A separate strategy.

A separate programme.

A separate set of people responsible for it.

"We support neurodiversity"

"We have an inclusion programme"

"We've done the training"

If those commitments don't change how work is structured, evaluated, or supported, they become reassurance rather than progress.

Inclusion that never alters the work itself isn't inclusion; it's comfort.

When systems ask too much of people

Most organisations don't need more fixes; they need better design.

It's worth noticing:

- Where people succeed *despite* the system rather than because of it
- Which processes rely on people compensating silently
- Where effort, care, or stabilising work goes unseen or unrewarded

Work shouldn't require constant self-translation just to be survivable.

Designing for humans means designing for variance, not treating difference as an edge case to be managed later.

The responsibility that can't stay vague

Design becomes exclusionary when ownership is unclear.

When no one is quite sure:

- Who owns system design
- What leaders are accountable for changing
- How success is measured beyond good intent
- What happens when a system causes harm

Responsibility diffuses.

And when responsibility diffuses, nothing really moves.

Being clear isn't about pointing fingers; it's about helping people make progress.

. . .

Small acts of leadership that matter

You don't need perfect alignment or a new mandate to lead differently.

Sometimes leadership looks like:

- Naming design debt when you see it, instead of normalising it
- Modelling flexibility without apology
- Protecting time for reflection, not just delivery
- Asking better questions instead of demanding faster answers

These moments aren't symbolic; they tell people what counts, and where it's safe to put their energy.

A final question worth sitting with

As you end the penultimate chapter of this book, ask yourself:

"If we were designing this system today, with what we now understand about people, work, and pressure, would we really build it this way?"

If the answer is no, that isn't a problem; it's useful information.

It tells you the system isn't broken, it's just outdated.

Work doesn't need to be redesigned for everyone; it needs to stop quietly working against some people.

That's how change happens, not through grand gestures, not overnight; but through small, deliberate choices, made with eyes wide open.

Conversation Starter:

"If we were designing our systems from scratch today, what would we do differently?"

Chapter 11

AI, automation, and the future we're quietly building

In January 2026, the World Economic Forum published a report with Accenture called *Proof over Promise*. It's based on hundreds of organisations sharing what AI is actually doing inside real workplaces.

And the takeaway isn't glamorous.

The organisations seeing results aren't the ones "buying AI"; they're the ones doing the boring bit: getting clear on the problem, fixing the plumbing, and designing the work around the people who have to live with it.

One example I loved was Cambridge Industries. They didn't build AI for a shiny innovation lab; they put it into the hands of the people doing the job.

Road inspectors take routine photos. The system spots damage, predicts where the road will deteriorate next, and helps teams prioritise repairs. On construction sites, drones flag safety risks and turn dense safety manuals into practical, site-specific guidance that can land through WhatsApp.

That's not sci-fi. That's work, made easier.

And the results were real: a 40% reduction in emergency road repair costs within six months, 3,000 AI-generated safety alerts, and a 50% reduction in safety incidents.

But again, the numbers only tell part of the story.

In people processes, this is what that kind of shift actually looks like.

In hiring, candidates aren't quietly screened out because they didn't phrase something "the right way".

The system surfaces potential and patterns, but humans still decide what matters.

In onboarding, new starters don't spend their first three months guessing what "good" looks like.

Expectations are visible. Feedback is timely. The basics aren't learned through mistakes.

In performance and progression, people don't have to perform confidence just to be seen.

Contribution is tracked through outcomes and evidence, not who speaks most in meetings.

In learning and development, support shows up when someone needs it, not six months later in a generic course.

People are guided, not labelled. Nudged, not monitored.

When AI is designed this way, it doesn't replace judgement.

It reduces the hidden work people do just to survive the system.

And that's the difference.

AI doesn't start by introducing new problems. It accelerates old ones.

There's a reason so many organisations feel like they're "doing AI" while seeing very little change in what work actually feels like. They've treated it like a tool purchase, when it's closer to a live redesign of how the organisation functions.

I was listening recently to a conversation between Matt Alder and Jonathan Kestenbaum (Managing Director at Alexander Mann Solutions - AMS) on the 'Recruiting Futures' podcast, and he captured it simply: buying an AI tool isn't the hard part. The hard part is what happens next.

Because AI doesn't just sit alongside people; it starts quietly eating into tasks, nudging responsibilities, shifting expectations, and changing the shape of jobs.

And unless the organisation has the muscle to keep redesigning work around that reality, "efficiency" stays private. Individuals might move faster, but the system doesn't learn. The organisation doesn't change. The same friction remains; just with a new layer of automation on top.

Technology doesn't fix systems; it reveals how they work when they're put under strain.

A well-known example came from Amazon. They built an AI tool to support hiring, trained on years of historical recruitment data. The system did exactly what it was designed to do: it learned from past decisions. The problem was that those past decisions reflected a workforce that was overwhelmingly male. So the AI quietly optimised for the same outcome, downgrading applications associated with women and reinforcing an imbalance that already existed. The tool wasn't broken; it was efficient in the wrong place.

That's the point many organisations miss.

If hiring already rewards confidence over capability, AI will optimise for confidence.

If performance is measured through narrow signals, AI will enforce those signals at scale.

If work already expects people to mask, perform, or conform, AI will reward the people who do that best.

None of this is theoretical.

It's already happening.

What's changed isn't the risk, it's the accessibility. These systems have been tested quietly, often in the background, by some of the largest and most powerful organisations in the world for years. What's new is how easily they can now be switched on by almost anyone.

What looks like progress from a distance can feel like pressure up close, especially when the systems underneath were fragile to begin with.

AI doesn't create these problems.

It just makes them harder to ignore.

When efficiency becomes the problem

AI is being deployed fastest where organisations feel the most strain:

- Recruitment
- Performance management
- Productivity tracking

- Learning and development

These are also the areas where people already experience the most friction.

I've warned before about mistaking speed for progress. Automating a flawed process doesn't fix it; it just removes friction for the organisation, not for the person inside it.

We've seen this before.

If a nurse becomes "more efficient" but has less time to notice distress, or a carer delivers tasks faster but with less presence, the system may look better while the outcome worsens.

The faster the system moves, the less space there is to notice what's wrong.

Efficiency that ignores human variation doesn't create fairness; it hides the damage that's being done.

The losers' loop

Over years of working inside HR, recruitment, and talent systems, I've come to an uncomfortable conclusion: we've been operating a long way below what these systems are actually capable of; not marginally, systemically.

I wouldn't put a neat percentage on it, but I've seen enough to be confident of this: large numbers of people end up in roles that don't fit them; not because they lack ability, but because our systems were never designed to recognise it in the first place.

What looks like meritocracy is often a loop.

People with weaker formal qualifications, patchy early careers, or the "wrong" signals attached to them, a postcode, a school, a company name that doesn't carry prestige, get filtered out early.

They don't land in high-quality environments where capability is developed, recognised, or compounded. Instead, they end up in lower-trust roles, poorer employers, or dead-end jobs with little investment in people.

From there, it becomes harder to escape the first impression the system has made about you.

Future employers don't see context; they see proxies. The CV now shows the "wrong" companies. The "wrong" trajectory. The "wrong" polish. So the better organisations won't take the risk. Not because the person isn't capable, but because the system reads their history as evidence of limitation rather than circumstance.

That's the losers' loop.

Once you're in it, every move reinforces the last. The system doesn't correct itself; it confirms itself.

HR and recruitment processes play a central role in maintaining this loop because they lean so heavily on inherited markers of worth. We reward continuity over recovery, pedigree over progress, confidence over competence; and we mistake defensibility for fairness.

This is why AI is such a moment of risk *and* opportunity.

AI will expose how flimsy many of these judgments are, but only if we let it. If we simply train models on historical hiring data, automate CV screening, or optimise for "successful profiles" without interrogating how success was defined, we will encode the losers' loop directly into software.

At that point, it doesn't just persist. It scales.

Bias by proxy becomes bias by design. Exclusion becomes efficient. Entire groups get quietly written out of opportunity; not through overt discrimination, but through perfectly rational-looking systems optimised on flawed assumptions.

We're not being asked to modernise a well-functioning wheel; we're being forced to rebuild one that was already buckled and broken.

AI can help us do that; but only if we stop using it to reinforce the past. The real work isn't making hiring faster or cheaper. It's redesigning systems that can recognise potential, context, and growth, and break cycles that were never fair to begin with.

Because if we get this wrong, AI won't fix inequality in work; it will automate it.

Where AI can genuinely help

This isn't an anti-AI argument.

Used well, AI can remove some of the invisible labour that quietly drains people at work.

For years, due to my dyslexia, and undiagnosed ADHD and autism, one of my biggest anxieties wasn't the conversation in a meeting. It was being asked to capture notes in real time, write on a whiteboard, or summarise actions while others watched.

The pressure didn't improve my contribution; it put me in a position where I would make more mistakes and feel less confident in the value I could offer.

The moment attention is split between thinking and performing competence, something is lost; often it's the best thinking in the room.

I see the same thing play out in other moments in the workplace.

I've worked with people who avoided asking questions in fast-moving discussions; not because they didn't understand, but because they needed more time to process and didn't want to be seen as slowing things down.

When ideas are captured, summarised, and shared after the fact, those voices re-enter the conversation. The quality of decisions improves, not because people changed, but because the system stopped excluding them by default.

I've also seen what happens when written communication is treated as a test of speed rather than clarity. When drafting, structuring, or sense-checking a message becomes less exposed, people contribute more thoughtfully; fewer misunderstandings, less rework, less quiet self-doubt.

Tools that transcribe, summarise, or structure information don't make people lazy; they remove fear, they free attention and allow energy to go into thinking, questioning, and contributing rather than self-monitoring and damage control.

This is the difference between being watched and being supported.

When AI carries some of the cognitive load that systems currently dump on individuals, it can widen participation rather than narrow it; but only if it's built that way.

The quiet ethical question leaders need to ask

The most important question about AI at work isn't *can we automate this?*

It's *who does this actually serve?*

If people can't see how decisions are being made, they stop challenging them.

If fit is reduced to a system, bias becomes harder to name.

And if work turns into constant monitoring, trust, and safety quietly disappears.

One of the most consequential decisions isn't whether AI is accurate; it's whether humans still have a way to question it.

I saw a very different version of this early on, when I worked for a background and reference checking startup.

At the time, it didn't look like a particularly exciting use of technology. It was hardly the glamorous end of recruitment. If anything, it was the part most people wanted to get through as quickly as possible.

But that was exactly the point.

Before automation, these checks were slow, manual, and fragile. Candidates waited weeks with no visibility.

References didn't come back. Compliance steps were delayed because one person was off sick or overwhelmed. Risk accumulated quietly on both sides.

They didn't automate judgement; they automated the delay.

The process became faster, clearer, and more transparent. Candidates could see what was happening. Organisations reduced risk in regulated environments. Nobody lost the ability to challenge decisions, because the decisions themselves were still human.

That's the balance leaders rarely talk about.

Ethical use of AI isn't about replacing people at the moments where judgement, context, and discretion matter most; it's about removing friction, uncertainty, and unnecessary risk from the parts of work that never needed human interpretation in the first place.

When AI is used to automate process, it often *restores* humanity.

When it's used to automate assessment, it quietly removes it.

So the ethical question isn't abstract.

It's practical.

Who benefits from this automation?

Who absorbs the cost when it fails?

And when something feels wrong, who still has the power to say so?

Those answers tell you far more about your use of AI than any policy ever will.

People as early signals, not edge cases

One pattern I see emerging is this: people who benefit most from well-designed systems are also the first to notice when systems fail.

Those who process, communicate, or recover differently often feel friction sooner; not because they are fragile, but because there is less spare capacity to absorb it. What others can work around, they must actively manage.

Many are already heavy users of AI tools; not out of novelty, but necessity. They use them to reduce friction, create structure, and manage overload.

They're not outliers; they're the first to feel when a system starts to fail.

When an AI tool overwhelms, constrains, or misreads people like this, it's rarely a niche problem; it's a sign the system itself is brittle.

Ignoring that warning sign doesn't just exclude a group; it weakens the system for everyone.

Design choices we'll live with for decades

Most of them don't arrive with a big announcement; they fall into place.

A performance metric added "for consistency".

A screening tool introduced "to save time".

An AI summary that quietly becomes the version people trust most.

None of these feel like big decisions in the moment.

But together, they start setting the rules.

- What counts as potential
- Who gets flagged as "high confidence"
- Whose work is visible without asking
- And whose contribution slowly fades because it doesn't travel well through the system

You see it when someone who stabilises a team never quite looks like a top performer on a dashboard; when pattern-spotting, risk-sensing, or deep specialist work gets flattened into a score.

When people adapt their behaviour not to do better work, but to fit what the system can recognise.

That's why "we'll come back and fix it later" isn't a helpful position.

By the time you notice the impact, people have already learned what gets rewarded and what doesn't.

They've changed how they speak in meetings, what they volunteer, what they stop bothering to offer at all.

AI isn't something that *might* shape work in the future; it's already shaping what gets amplified, what gets smoothed out, and what gets ignored.

The real question isn't whether AI will change work; it's whether organisations are willing to take responsibility for the shape they're giving it.

Responsibility, not fear

This chapter isn't a warning sign.

It should be a line in the sand.

Not about panicking.

About owning the decisions already being made.

Every tool introduced changes in behaviour:

What people prioritise.

What they optimise for.

What they stop doing because it no longer "counts".

Leaders don't need to become technologists.

But they do need to recognise that inaction carries consequences.

Choosing a tool is choosing a direction, even when it's sold as efficiency, innovation, or progress.

AI doesn't only reshape tasks. It increases the rate at which people must adapt. When stability isn't designed in, that constant reorientation looks like engagement, until it quietly becomes exhaustion.

Because the future of work isn't being decided by AI.

It's being shaped, quietly and deliberately, by the humans who decide what to adopt, what to measure, and what to ignore.

And responsibility doesn't start when something goes wrong; it starts at the moment a system is switched on.

A final truth to leave with you

If work hasn't been designed for humans yet, AI won't fix that.

But if organisations are willing to reduce friction, widen participation, and be clearer about what really matters,

AI could help them do it more consistently, and at scale.

The future won't judge us by the tools we adopted; it will judge us by the systems we chose to build with them.

Designed for Human Action

(How to avoid automating the wrong signals)

AI and automation don't come with purpose.

They don't have a set of values.

They take on the priorities they're given.

What we're building now will shape who gets seen, supported, promoted, filtered out, or quietly exhausted in the years ahead.

Not because technology decides to, but because existing assumptions get built into the code.

This chapter isn't asking you to predict the future; it's asking you to take responsibility for the direction of travel.

When speed gets mistaken for progress

There's a strong pull towards faster systems.

Faster decisions.

Faster screening.

Faster performance signals.

Speed feels like momentum.

But when efficiency becomes the primary measure of success, human complexity starts to look like friction.

Difference gets flattened.

Context gets lost.

The most harmful systems rarely announce themselves as harmful.

They arrive under reassuring labels like *optimisation*, *streamlining*, or *scale*.

Where judgement still matters

The most important design question isn't what AI can replace.

It's where judgement still belongs.

It's worth pausing to ask:

- Where does nuance change the outcome?
- Where does context matter more than consistency?

- Where would a wrong decision carry human consequences, not just operational ones?

Technology should support thinking, not remove responsibility for it.

If no one can explain why a system made a decision, that system is already doing too much.

What can't stay invisible

AI becomes risky when its role fades into the background.

When people don't know:

- Where automation is being used
- What inputs shape decisions
- Who is accountable when outcomes are wrong
- Which values override efficiency

Transparency doesn't get in the way of innovation; it reveals problems before they become embedded.

When systems aren't understood, people either over-trust them or work around them.

Both increase risk.

Neither is safe or fair.

. . .

What to hold lightly

Tools will change.

Models will improve.

Certainty will be promised.

All of that should be held lightly.

What matters more are the principles underneath:

- Human review over blind trust
- Support over surveillance
- Enablement over extraction

When a tool no longer reflects those principles, it begins to shape behaviour in ways leaders didn't choose.

Those effects accumulate, quietly at first, then unmistakably.

A question worth sitting with

Before you move on, sit with this:

"If this system scaled perfectly, who would it quietly exclude, and would we notice?"

Because the future of work won't be shaped by the technology we adopt; it will be shaped by the assumptions we allow to mould into design.

Staying human isn't about resisting progress; it's about choosing it deliberately.

Conversation Starter:

"How might our use of technology unintentionally reinforce old assumptions or barriers?"

Chapter 12
Designed to last

Work doesn't usually fail people all at once.

It fails them slowly:

Through small moments that are easy to explain away.

Through systems that mostly work, until they don't.

Through expectations that feel reasonable, until the cost of meeting them becomes invisible.

That's what this book has been about.

Not pointing fingers.

Not assigning blame.

Not asking organisations to become something they're not.

It's been about noticing what we've normalised:

When people struggle quietly.

When capability is missed because it doesn't present itself in familiar ways.

When energy is spent surviving systems rather than doing meaningful work.

None of this happens because leaders don't care; it happens because most systems are inherited, reused, and rarely questioned once they're in place, especially when they appear to be working for the people in charge of them.

And once something becomes "just how we do things", it stops being examined as a choice.

Seeing the system changes the conversation

Once you start looking at work through a design lens, it makes all the difference.

You notice where confidence is rewarded more than contribution:

Where clarity is expected rather than provided.

Where flexibility exists in theory, but not in practice.

Where people are praised for resilience when what they really need is support.

You also start to notice something else:

Many of the people labelled as "difficult", "inconsistent", or "not quite fitting" are often the first to expose where the system is weak.

They're not breaking the system; they're revealing it.

As we discussed in earlier in the book, people who've faced systemic barriers, tend to surface these cracks earlier because the margin for error is smaller. But the underlying design issues affect far more people than we usually admit.

That's why this conversation matters beyond diversity and inclusion.

For a long time, in life and in work, I assumed the problem was me.

I was capable. I delivered. I learned the rules eventually. From the outside, nothing looked broken. And because nothing looked broken, there was nothing to fix.

What I didn't have language for then was how much effort it took just to stay level. The preparation no one saw. The recovery time that quietly disappeared. The constant scanning of environments to work out what was expected, what was safe to say, and what wasn't.

It wasn't dramatic. There was no single incident to point to. Just a steady, low-level friction that followed me from role to role. And because I could cope, the system never had to change.

Years later, I found myself in a different kind of environment. Not perfect. Not unusually kind. Just slightly better designed.

Expectations were clearer. Decisions were written down. Questions weren't treated as interruptions. Pace varied without apology. The important things were named early instead of inferred late.

Nothing about my ability changed.

What changed was the cost.

The same work took less out of me. I didn't need to over-prepare to protect myself from misunderstanding. I stopped replaying conversations on the way home or through the night. I had more left at the end of the day; not because the work was easier, but because it wasn't asking me to compensate for what the system hadn't thought through.

That's when it became impossible to unsee what had been happening all along.

The struggle I'd internalised as personal wasn't random. It was predictable. It followed the design.

When work relies on unspoken rules, constant self-regulation, and quiet endurance, the people who feel it first aren't weaker. They're closer to the edge of what the system demands. They reveal the strain earlier because they have less margin to absorb it.

Nothing about this required heroics. No culture programme. No overhaul. Just fewer assumptions left hanging in the air.

That experience didn't make me optimistic about work.

It made me clearer.

Clear that when people do well only by spending themselves, the system is being propped up by invisible effort. Clear that when performance improves because friction is removed, not pressure added, ability hasn't been unlocked, it's been allowed to show up.

And clear that if we keep asking individuals to carry what design could carry instead, we'll keep mistaking coping for competence, and silence for sustainability.

The question, then, isn't whether people can adapt.

They always have.

The question is how much of themselves they're being asked to spend just to belong.

Inclusion isn't a programme. It's something organisations must learn how to do

One of the biggest myths in workplace inclusion is that it can be delivered through policy, training, or good intent alone.

Policies describe what *should* happen.

Training raises awareness.

Intent sets tone.

But none of them redesign the work itself.

Inclusion becomes real when systems change how people experience work from day to day.

- How they're assessed
- How they're onboarded
- How expectations are set
- How feedback is given
- How progression happens

When those systems stay the same, inclusion becomes something people talk about rather than something they feel.

That gap is where trust erodes.

Leadership after awareness

Once you see how design shapes outcomes, standing still isn't passive; it keeps things exactly as they are.

Continuing to use systems that quietly exclude isn't usually intentional.

But it is still a choice.

Leadership, in this context, isn't about having all the answers; it's about being willing to ask better questions.

Questions like:

- What effort are people expending here that we never see
- Who thrives easily, and who succeeds despite the system
- Where are we asking individuals to adapt instead of adapting the design

These aren't comfortable questions; but they're necessary ones.

Because the cost of ignoring them doesn't disappear; it just gets absorbed by people, one by one.

Designing work that fits humans

Designing for humans doesn't mean lowering standards; it means being clearer about what matters.

It means separating signal from noise, ability from performance theatre, contribution from confidence.

It means recognising that consistency doesn't require sameness, and fairness doesn't come from pretending difference doesn't exist.

Most importantly, it means accepting that systems are never finished.

They either evolve intentionally, or they calcify around outdated assumptions.

Work that is designed to last is work that can change.

A final question

As you close this book, there's one question worth taking forward:

"When people do well here, is the system supporting them, or are they supporting the system?"

That question doesn't demand urgency.

It doesn't require perfection.

But it does require ownership.

Because once you start designing work for humans,

everything else begins to make more sense.

And quietly, deliberately, things start to change.

My final thought; Right Here, Right Now!

Where real change usually starts.

It's easy to assume that the future lies somewhere far away:

In breakthroughs.

In laboratories.

In self-driving cars, rockets, and systems so complex they feel almost abstract.

We're surrounded by stories that tell us innovation is always loud, shiny, and spectacular; that progress arrives from above, fully formed, and changes everything at once.

But that isn't how change usually shows up in real life.

One of my favourite examples comes from graphene, first isolated at the University of Manchester. For years, it was talked about as the material that would transform everything; flexible screens, aerospace, medical breakthroughs. The stuff of headlines and keynote slides.

Some of that will still happen.

But one of graphene's earliest, most practical impacts wasn't in space or high-end tech; it was in something far more ordinary: recycling tyres.

Normally, every time rubber is recycled, its quality degrades. Add graphene, and something unexpected happens: the material improves. Old tyres become more durable products. Things like mats, flooring, everyday items that don't look revolutionary at all.

It wasn't glamorous.

It wasn't what anyone predicted.

But it made a real, measurable difference.

That isn't a failure of innovation, it's how innovation works.

And it's the same in work.

For all the noise around AI, automation, and transformation, the biggest opportunities aren't always where the spotlight is pointing; they're often in the most ordinary, overlooked parts of working life.

Onboarding that actually sets people up properly. Expectations that are clear instead of implied. Systems that stop leaking effort. Managers who aren't left to compensate for broken design.

These aren't headline-grabbing changes.

But they're the ones that change lives.

Part of what drove me to write this book was the growing gap between how the future of work is talked about and how work is actually experienced.

The articles, panels, and product launches rarely reflect the daily reality of people trying to do their jobs. The pressure. The exclusions. The quiet adaptations. The energy spent navigating systems that weren't designed with them in mind.

We talk about innovation as if it lives somewhere "out there", while ignoring how much work still happens under conditions that are poorly designed, unnecessarily rigid, or quietly harmful.

We still haven't solved unemployment.

We still waste enormous human capability.

We still see people excluded, stalled, or burned out, not because they lack skill, but because the system around them makes progress harder than it needs to be.

And yet, we're told the future has arrived.

If the future of work is here, then the question becomes unavoidable:

Who is it working for?

Because no matter how advanced the technology becomes, humans are still at the centre of every system. We decide what gets measured, what gets rewarded, what gets ignored. We choose whether tools reduce friction or amplify it, whether they widen participation or narrow it.

AI won't fix work that was never designed properly.

But it will make those design choices more visible; and more consequential.

That's why this isn't a book about fearing technology.

And it isn't a book about worshipping it either.

It's about remembering that meaningful change rarely starts with the rocket; it starts with the rubber mat.

With the unglamorous work of fixing what's already in front of us.

With asking whether people are carrying effort the system should be carrying instead.

With designing environments where more people can contribute without burning out, masking, or being quietly filtered out.

If we can get those basics right, then the more complex innovations have something solid to sit on.

If we can't, no amount of intelligence, artificial or otherwise, will save us from repeating the same mistakes at scale.

The future of work doesn't need to be imagined; it needs to be redesigned:

Slowly.

Deliberately.

Human by human.

And if we're serious about building something that lasts, that's where we start.

Those dreams we set free down the river, into the
sea, were never lost, only waiting to be.

Like the water that rests in the ocean below, then rises
unseen, waiting to let go.

Lifted to sky, to wander, to roam, to fall again gently, far
from its home.

The rain meets the land, the soil, the tree, and carries old
stories reborn to be.

So too with our ideas, released from our sight, they drift
through the world, through time, through light.

They fall to new hands, new minds, new dreams, flowing
once more from the land to the river and into the sea.

Bibliography

This section lists key works, articles, and resources that have informed the thinking and arguments in Designed for Humans. It is not exhaustive, but highlights foundational texts and recommended further reading for those interested in rethinking work, inclusion, neurodiversity, and the impact of AI on organisations.

References & Further Reading

- Kirby, A. & Smith, T. (2021). *Neurodiversity at Work: Drive Innovation, Performance and Productivity with a Neurodiverse Workforce*. Kogan Page. A foundational text on neurodiversity and workplace inclusion.

- Silberman, S. (2015). *NeuroTribes: The Legacy of Autism and the Future of Neurodiversity*. Avery. A landmark work on the history and future of neurodiversity.

- Austin, R. D. & Pisano, G. P. (2017). Neurodiversity as a Competitive Advantage. *Harvard Business Review*, May–June. Influential article on the business case for neurodiversity.

- Bourke, J. & Dillon, B. (2018). *The Diversity and Inclusion Revolution: Eight Powerful Truths*. Deloitte. Research-driven insights on inclusion and organisational change.

- Maslach, C. & Leiter, M. P. (1997). *The Truth About Burnout*. Jossey-Bass. Classic work on burnout and workplace wellbeing.

- Brown, B. (2018). *Dare to Lead*. Random House. Leadership, vulnerability, and building inclusive cultures.

- Brown, T. (2009). *Change by Design: How Design Thinking Transforms Organizations and Inspires Innovation*. HarperBusiness. Design thinking applied to organisational transformation.

Bibliography

- Kahneman, D. (2011). *Thinking, Fast and Slow*. Farrar, Straus and Giroux. Seminal work on human decision-making and cognitive bias.

- Bock, L. (2015). *Work Rules!*. Twelve. Insights from Google's former SVP of People Operations on hiring and culture.

- Scott, K. (2017). *Radical Candor*. St. Martin's Press. Practical guidance on feedback, trust, and communication at work.

- Lencioni, P. (2002). *The Five Dysfunctions of a Team*. Jossey-Bass. Team dynamics and organisational health.

- Hewlett, S. A. (2013). *Forget a Mentor, Find a Sponsor*. Harvard Business Review Press. The role of sponsorship in career progression.

- Ibarra, H. (2015). *Act Like a Leader, Think Like a Leader*. Harvard Business Review Press. Leadership identity and career growth.

- Senge, P. (2006). *The Fifth Discipline*. Currency. Systems thinking for organisational learning and change.

- Edmondson, A. (2018). *The Fearless Organization*. Wiley. Psychological safety and high-performing teams.

- Eubanks, V. (2018). *Automating Inequality*. St. Martin's Press. The social impact of automation and algorithmic decision-making.

- Noble, S. U. (2018). *Algorithms of Oppression*. NYU Press. How bias is embedded in search engines and algorithms.

- Oleeo & Aptitude Research. (2025). *Setting the Standard for Responsible AI: A Guide for Modern Recruiters*. Responsible AI in recruitment and HR.

- Brill, J. & Wunker, S. (2025). *AI and the Octopus Organization: Building the Superintelligent Firm*. AI, organisational design, and the future of intelligent firms.

- Smith, T. (2026). Why the Best Hires Never Apply. *LinkedIn Article*. On hidden talent and systemic hiring barriers.

- Smith, T. (2026). If you need a six-month probation, the

problem isn't the employee. *LinkedIn Newsletter.* Rethinking onboarding, trust, and performance assessment.

- Lee, H. (2025). Recruiting Brainfood – Issue 477. *Recruiting Brainfood*, November. Trends and debates in recruiting and talent.

- *Neurodiversity with Theo Smith.* Podcast. Conversations on neurodiversity, inclusion, and the future of work.

- *Neurodiversity with Theo Smith: Mima & John – From Manager to Mentor.* Podcast episode. A practical conversation on inclusive management and neurodiversity in action.

- Norman, D. (2013). *The Design of Everyday Things.* Basic Books. A foundational design text arguing that when people struggle, the failure lies in the system or interface — not the individual.

- Perrow, C. (1984). *Normal Accidents.* Princeton University Press. How complex systems fail in predictable ways, even when individuals act competently and in good faith.

- Scott, J. C. (1998). *Seeing Like a State.* Yale University Press. An exploration of how systems optimised for efficiency and legibility often erase human complexity, local knowledge, and lived experience.

- O'Neil, C. (2016). *Weapons of Math Destruction.* Crown. A critique of opaque algorithms and data-driven systems that scale bias while appearing neutral and objective.

- Criado Perez, C. (2019). *Invisible Women.* Chatto & Windus. A powerful design parallel showing how systems built around a narrow "default" human systematically exclude others.

- McKinsey & Company. Organisational health and systems effectiveness research. Widely cited management research on how organisational design, decision-making systems, and structural friction shape performance and outcomes.

www.ingramcontent.com/pod-product-compliance
Lightning Source LLC
Chambersburg PA
CBHW031957050726
47590CB00006B/1937